God of Our Fathers

Advice and Prayers
Of Our Nation's Founders

Compiled and Edited by
Josiah Benjamin Richards

Reading Books
Reading, Pennsylvania

Reading Books
526 Washington Street
P. O. Box 1456
Reading, PA 19603-1456

God of Our Fathers:
Advice and Prayers of Our Nation's Founders

United States — History
Quotations
Church and State — United States
Political Science — United States — History

Printed in the United States of America
ISBN 0-9643679-1-2

Contents

CONTENTS CONTINUED ON NEXT PAGE

Brief Biographies of Our Nation's Founders

Why This Book is Important

This book contains the advice and prayers of our nation's founders — in their own words. An understanding of the spiritual aspect of their lives, as revealed in the following quotations, is important because it guided the actions of the remarkable individuals who established the United States. Reverence for God was a matter of significance for each of them. That reverence influenced the American Revolution and the Constitution of the United States. It was the driving force behind the First Amendment, which guarantees freedom of religion to all of us.

American history is incomplete without honest recognition of the spiritual concerns of the early leaders of our nation. Unfortunately, their reverence for God has been quietly excluded from most books in recent years. This is especially true of school texts. Setting the record straight is important.

A Valuable Schoolbook

Although the language of some quotations is somewhat demanding, this book is appropriate for secondary school students, as well as for adult readers. To facilitate its use as a schoolbook, 180 quotations — one for each day of instruction in most communities — are presented in the central section. The short specialized chapters toward the back include numerous additional statements by our nation's founders that may be substituted for the 180 basic quotations.

For all readers, the advice and prayers on the following pages will be most thoroughly appreciated when a single selection is considered each day.

The supplementary volume, *Historical Background and Sources for Parents and Teachers: For Use with the Advice and Prayers of Our Nation's Founders*, includes detailed citations, a summary of important events for the years 1725 through 1825, extensive biographies of the most influential leaders of the period, and brief definitions of key words.

How This Book Began

Some time ago, a search for a general reference book combining two of my son's interests — religion (his undergraduate major) and history (his current graduate study) — ended in disappointment. No collection of statements by our nation's founders with respect to God and spiritual matters was readily available. Even bookstores in and around Independence Hall offered no volume of this kind.

Was it possible that such important ideas by such significant figures in American history had never been compiled? The standard answer was: "Apparently so. We don't have anything like that." But why? The response to this second question was consistent: "Lack of material, I guess. They probably didn't say much about God."

That answer seemed to be just plain wrong, based on even the most casual review of American history.

Benjamin Franklin's call for prayer during the Constitutional Convention is well known. However, finding the specific quotation proved a bit difficult.

George Washington pointed out the connection between religion, morality and the happiness of a nation in his often quoted Farewell Address, but the exact words are no longer easy to locate.

James Madison, the key figure in the development of our Constitution and Bill of Rights, referred to "the duty which we owe to our Creator" and expressed his opinion that belief in God "is essential to the moral order of the world and to the happiness of man." Thomas Jefferson, Madison's mentor, wrote to a friend that "God has formed us moral agents" and advised his grandson: "Adore God." Why are these quotations not readily available today?

That question led to a more thorough search, which gradually grew into a project — a project that has become this book: a collection of the spiritual statements and virtuous advice of our nation's founders. Included are personal prayers, family letters, correspondence with friends and official proclamations of the men who took the lead in establishing the United States.

A Note on Editing

This edition is intended to enable young readers, as well as the general public, to grasp the substance of the writings of our nation's founders. It is not designed to serve the formal requirements of advanced scholarship.

Old style spellings (and misspellings), unusual or archaic capitalization, and outmoded or idiosyncratic punctuation have been edited, where necessary for clarity, in conformity with current conventions. In rare instances, a modern synonym has been substituted for a word that has undergone a significant change of meaning (such as "unselfish" for "disinterested," which is now often confused with "uninterested," or "fanaticism" for "enthusiasm" in a specific context).

The sole purpose of condensing the text, where indicated, has been to convey the ideas of the founders in the fewest words. Preserving essential meaning — the original intent of each writer — has been the fundamental standard for determining the nature of the edits.

In some instances, the authors of passages in this book addressed more than one aspect of a basic spiritual topic in a single letter, proclamation or essay. Such multifaceted commentaries have, in most cases, been pruned to deal with a single issue: the essential relationship between God and man acting in history, or the importance of virtue in education and public life. Most theological controversies and sectarian niceties have been excluded.

The complete source of every quotation will be found in the supplementary volume, *Historical Background and Sources for Parents and Teachers: For Use with The Advice and Prayers of Our Nation's Founders*.

Acknowledgements

Hundreds of individuals who have laid the foundation for this book during the last two hundred years cannot be acknowledged by name. They include the archivists, researchers, manuscript compilers, catalogers, assistant editors and others who have helped to bring together the writings of our nation's founders. Their essential work is greatly appreciated.

The historians, librarians and other personnel of Independence National Historical Park, the American Philosophical Society, the Reading Public Library, the Free Library of Philadelphia, the Historical Society of Pennsylvania and the Library Company of Philadelphia were extremely generous with their time and professional knowledge. Anna Coxe Toogood and Roy E. Goodman provided especially helpful guidance.

Individuals who have contributed valuable ideas throughout this project include Christopher V. Brown, William H. Connor, Robert J. Daras, The Rev. Charles E. Fair, Joseph N. Farrell, Douglas T. Hicks, Joshua A. Miller, Karen A. Miller and Barbara T. Nudelman. Their support is gratefully acknowledged.

Kathleen Bieber McNally is due special thanks for her encouragement and her coordination of the production process. Appreciation is also extended to Liza Alvarado for her word processing work and to Elizabeth Jensen for her editorial suggestions.

The greatest acknowledgement must be given to our nation's founders, who wrote the words and performed the deeds that made our liberty possible. They would, in turn, acknowledge the Divine Author of All Blessings.

Advice and Prayers

Of Our Nation's Founders

It is that particular Wise and good God, who is the author and owner of our system, that I propose for the object of my praise and adoration.

He is not above caring for us, being pleased with our praise and offended when we slight Him or neglect his Glory....

I love Him therefore for his goodness, and I adore Him for his wisdom.

Let me then not fail to praise my God continually, for it is His due, and it is all I can return for His many favors and great goodness to me; and let me resolve to be virtuous, that I may be happy, that I may please Him.

Benjamin Franklin
"First Principles"
(Personal Papers)
November 20, 1728

At the age of 22, Benjamin Franklin prepared this guide to personal devotion, a practice he continued daily throughout his life.

For peace and liberty, for food and raiment, for corn, and wine, and milk, and every kind of healthful nourishment, — Good God, I thank thee!

For the common benefits of air and light; for useful fire and delicious water, — Good God, I thank thee!

For knowledge, and literature, and every useful art, for my friends and their prosperity, and for the fewness of my enemies, — Good God, I thank thee!

For all thy innumerable benefits; for life, and reason, and the use of speech; for health, and joy, and every pleasant hour, — My good God, I thank thee!

Benjamin Franklin
"Thanks"
(Personal Papers)
November 20, 1728

Benjamin Franklin cultivated the habit of giving praise to God. As the elder statesman of the Constitutional Convention — nearly sixty years after he wrote this devotional guide — he called for opening each session with a prayer.

We should love and revere the Deity for his goodness, and thank Him for his benefits; we should adore Him for his wisdom, fear Him for his power, and pray to Him for his favor and protection. And this religion will be a powerful regulator of our actions, give us peace and tranquility within our own minds and render us benevolent, useful and beneficial to others.

> Benjamin Franklin
> Lecture on the Providence of God
>   in the Government of the World
> 1729

Benjamin Franklin clearly regarded "the Deity" as a personal God deserving of reverent prayer — and he shared his ideas on this vital subject with others. Because he was born many years before the other founders of this nation, Franklin's writings represent the first six quotations in this book.

There is one God, who made all things. He governs the world by his providence. He ought to be worshiped by adoration, prayer, and thanksgiving. The most acceptable service of God is doing good to man. The soul is immortal. God will certainly reward virtue and punish vice, either here or hereafter.

Benjamin Franklin
Autobiography
1731

Soon to become a world-famous scientist, Benjamin Franklin carefully examined all aspects of life. This observation, made at 25 years of age, was recalled in his autobiography written forty years later.

To God we owe fear and love; to our neighbors justice and character; to ourselves prudence and sobriety.

Benjamin Franklin
Poor Richard's Almanac
September, 1745

Benjamin Franklin's ideas were most widely circulated in Poor Richard's Almanac, *which he published annually from 1732 to 1758. The success of the almanac, his newspaper (*The Pennsylvania Gazette), *and his printing company enabled him to retire from active business in 1748, at age 42.*

May the God of Wisdom, Strength, and Power, the Lord of the Armies of Israel, inspire us with prudence in this time of danger; take away from us all the seeds of contention and division, and unite the hearts and counsels of all of us, of whatever sect or nation, in one bond of peace, brotherly love, and generous public spirit.   May He give us strength and resolution to amend our lives, and remove from among us every thing that is displeasing to Him; afford us His most gracious protection, confound the designs of our enemies, and give peace in all our borders.

Benjamin Franklin
Plain Truth
November 14, 1747

This passage was written during King George's War (the Third Intercolonial War between Britain and France) when attacks by the French and their Native American allies were widely feared.   In fact, Benjamin Franklin organized the Pennsylvania militia to defend the frontier, then less than 75 miles from Philadelphia.

Suppose a nation in some distant region should take the Bible for their only law book, and every member should regulate his conduct by the precepts exhibited there. Every member would be obliged in conscience to temperance and frugality and industry, to justice and kindness and charity towards his fellow men, and to piety and love, and reverence towards almighty God. In this Commonwealth, no man would impair his health by gluttony, drunkenness, or lust — no man would steal or lie or any way defraud his neighbor, but would live in peace and good will with all men — no man would blaspheme his Maker or profane his worship, but a rational and manly, a sincere and unaffected piety and devotion, would reign in all hearts.

John Adams
Diary
February 22, 1756

This entry in the diary of John Adams was written at age 21, while teaching school after graduating from Harvard College. He continued to write about God and prayer throughout his life, which was devoted to public service from the early days of the Continental Congress in the mid-1770s through four years as the second President of the United States in the late 1790s.

[God] has connected the greatest pleasure with the discovery of truth, and made it our interest to pursue with eagerness these intense pleasures. Have we not the greatest reason, then, yea, is it not our indispensable duty, to return our sincere love and gratitude to this greatest, kindest, and most profuse Benefactor? Would it not show the deepest baseness and most infamous ingratitude to scorn or to disregard a being to whose inexhausted beneficence we are so deeply indebted?

John Adams
Diary
August 22, 1756

Nearly twenty years before he wrote a resolution for a day of fasting and prayer for the Continental Congress, John Adams gave careful consideration to religious duty.

There is no rank in natural knowledge of equal dignity and importance with that of being a good parent, a good child, and good husband or wife, a good neighbor or friend, a good subject or citizen, that is, in short, a good Christian.

Benjamin Franklin
Letter to Miss Mary Stevenson
June 11, 1760

A citizen of the Colony founded by the ecumenical William Penn, Benjamin Franklin rarely mentioned particular religious preferences. He did not wish to appear to support one sect above another, which was then the government policy in England and many of the American Colonies.

9

The power of God Almighty is the power that can properly and strictly be called supreme and absolute. In the order of nature immediately under him comes the power of a simple democracy.

James Otis
The Rights of the British Colonies Asserted and Proved
1764

A convincing speaker and forceful writer, James Otis was Boston's spokesman against the British use of "writs of assistance," general search warrants that were backed up by the Royal Navy as part of a new tax collection effort in Massachusetts in the early 1760s. He is best known for his declaration that "taxation without representation is tyranny."

God is very good to us. Let us enjoy His favors with a thankful and cheerful heart; and, as we can make no direct return to him, show our sense of His goodness to us, by continuing to do good to our fellow creatures, without regarding the returns they make us. The friendships of this world are changeable, uncertain, transitory things; but His favor, if we can secure it, is an inheritance forever.

> Benjamin Franklin
> Letter to Mrs. Deborah Franklin
> June 4, 1765

Benjamin Franklin was in London, England as a representative of Pennsylvania during the crisis provoked by the Stamp Act. After the British Parliament imposed a tax on the American Colonies by requiring that all legal documents bear revenue stamps, a great outcry arose from Massachusetts to Georgia. The Act was repealed the next year after Franklin was invited to Parliament to present the American cause.

And if a [government official] shall usurp the supreme and absolute government of America, and set up his instructions as laws ... who will presume to say that the people have not a right — or that it is not their indispensable duty to God and their country, by all rational means in their power — to resist them?

Samuel Adams
Letter to *The Boston Gazette*
October 14, 1771

During 1771, Boston businessman Samuel Adams continued to promote the Patriot cause while most American leaders were temporarily silenced by the previous year's repeal of nearly all of the import taxes that had been imposed by the British Parliament in 1767. Only a tax on tea remained from the "Townshend measures," named for the prime minister at that time.

Conceiving God to be the fountain of wisdom, I thought it right and necessary to solicit his assistance for obtaining it. To this end I formed the following little prayer, which was prefixed to my tables of examination, for daily use.

"O powerful Goodness! Bountiful Father! Merciful Guide! Increase in me that wisdom which discovers my truest interest. Strengthen my resolutions to perform what that wisdom dictates. Accept my kind offices to thy other children as the only return in my power for thy continual favors to me."

Benjamin Franklin
Autobiography
1771

As America's most renowned personality, Benjamin Franklin shared some of his previously private beliefs with the public.

Merciful God! Inspire thy people with wisdom and fortitude, and direct them to gracious ends.... The religion and public liberty of a people are intimately connected; their interests are interwoven, they cannot subsist separately; and therefore they rise and fall together. For this reason, it is always observable, that those who are combined to destroy the people's liberties, practice every art to poison their morals. How greatly then does it concerns us to put a stop to the progress of tyranny.

Samuel Adams
Letter to *The Boston Gazette*
October 5, 1772

As New England's chief spokesman and street organizer for the Patriot cause, Samuel Adams had become a relentless critic of the British presence in America. Although an articulate Harvard graduate like his cousin John, Samuel Adams (the holder of a Master of Arts degree) earned his living as a brewer and local tax collector.

A watchful eye must be kept on ourselves lest while we are building ideal monuments of renown and bliss here [on earth] we neglect to have our names enrolled in the annals of Heaven.

James Madison
Letter to William Bradford
November 9, 1772

Shortly after graduating from college, James Madison revealed his motivation for the life of public service that he would soon begin. Fifteen years later, he became the organizing force in the drafting and ratification of the Constitution of the United States. Following service in the first Congress and as Secretary of State in Thomas Jefferson's administration, he was elected our fourth President.

The right to freedom [is] the gift of God Almighty.... The Rights of the Colonists as Christians ... may be best understood by reading — and carefully studying — the institutes of the great Lawgiver and head of the Christian Church: which are to be found clearly written and promulgated in the New Testament.

Samuel Adams
The Rights of the Colonists
(Resolution Adopted
    by the Town of Boston)
November 20, 1772

In 1772, the people of America openly expressed their belief in a direct connection between freedom and God.

We join ... in supplicating Almighty God for his direction, assistance and blessing in every laudable effort that may be made for the securing to ourselves and posterity the free and full enjoyment of those precious rights and privileges for which our renowned forefathers expended so much treasure and blood.

> Samuel Adams
> Committee of Correspondence of
>   Boston to the Town of Rowley
> April 7, 1773

Much as we now look to Samuel Adams and the other leaders of his generation for inspiration, he expressed his gratitude for the sacrifices of his forefathers.

Providence seems by every means intent on making us a great people. May our virtues public and private grow with us, and be durable — that liberty, civil and religious, may be secured to our posterity....

Benjamin Franklin
Letter to Samuel Mather
July 7, 1773

Having returned to London to represent Pennsylvania and three other Colonies in trade and legal matters, Benjamin Franklin attempted to find a reasonable basis for agreement between Britain and the Americans. He was ultimately unsuccessful and became a signer of the Declaration of Independence.

The God who gave us life, gave us liberty at the same time: the hand of force may destroy, but cannot disjoin them.

> Thomas Jefferson
> Instructions to the Virginia Delegates
>   in the Continental Congress (Draft)
> July, 1774

By his early thirties, Thomas Jefferson had developed a highly effective writing style which he put to good use in the Patriot cause. Two years later, he would be called upon to prepare the Declaration of Independence.

The all wise Creator of man impressed certain laws on his nature. A desire of happiness, and of society, are two of those laws. They were not intended to destroy, but to support each other. Man has therefore a right to promote the best union of both, in order to enjoy both in the highest degree.

John Dickinson
"An Essay" Communicating
    Instructions from Pennsylvania
    to Other Colonies
July, 1774

John Dickinson was known as "the Penman of the Revolution" for his wide range of writings on behalf of American rights, beginning with his Letters from a Pennsylvania Farmer, which were widely read in England and throughout the Colonies. He prepared resolutions and messages for the Pennsylvania Assembly and wrote a popular "Liberty Song" that supported the cause of the Patriots.

It is an indispensable duty which we owe to God, our country, ourselves and posterity, by all lawful ways and means in our power to maintain, defend and preserve those civil and religious rights and liberties, for which many of our fathers fought, bled and died, and to hand them down entire to future generations.

Suffolk County, Massachusetts
  (Town Meeting)
Resolution
September 6, 1774

During 1774, beliefs concerning rights and liberties were collectively expressed as resolutions. The determination of Americans to defend their cause grew accordingly.

The sacred rights of mankind are not to be rummaged for among old parchments or musty records. They are written, as with a sunbeam, in the whole volume of human nature, by the Hand of the Divinity itself, and can never be erased or obscured by mortal power.

Alexander Hamilton
"The Farmer Refuted"
February 5, 1775

Before turning twenty years of age, Alexander Hamilton had dedicated his persuasive speaking and writing style to promoting the rights of the American Colonies. The year before this passage was written, he had energized a large public meeting in New York with his well crafted arguments and determined delivery, and then began to write extensively in pamphlets and newspaper essays.

The Supreme Being gave existence to man, together with the means of preserving and beautifying that existence. He endowed him with rational faculties, by the help of which to discern and pursue such things as were consistent with his duty and interest; and invested him with an inviolable right to personal liberty and personal safety.

Alexander Hamilton
"The Farmer Refuted"
February 5, 1775

Only rarely did Alexander Hamilton make public statements about God and duty. Throughout his comparatively brief life, during which he exerted important influence in ratification of the United States Constitution and served as the first Secretary of the Treasury under President Washington, he expressed concern that the ordinary citizen would have insufficient regard for the importance of sound government and would forfeit the principles of the American Revolution and the Constitution.

This Union among the Colonies and warmth of affection can be attributed to nothing less than the agency of the Supreme Being. If we believe that He superintends and directs the great affairs of empires, we have reason to expect the restoration ... of the public liberties, unless by our own misconduct we have rendered ourselves unworthy of it; for He certainly wills the happiness of those of his creatures who deserve it, and without public liberty, we cannot be happy.

> Samuel Adams
> Letter to "A Southern Friend"
> March 12, 1775

Samuel Adams and John Hancock would soon have to flee Massachusetts — with advance warning from Paul Revere during his midnight ride to alert the "Minutemen" at Concord that British troops were advancing from Boston. Adams and Hancock narrowly escaped arrest for "high treason" and quickly made their way to the Continental Congress in Philadelphia.

The affections of the Deity are universally extended.... The object of this government is the happiness of the governed, not of those who govern merely. We will in no respect lose sight of this great object. God, nature, honor, duty, our happiness and our children's happiness, all forbid it.

James Iredell
The Principles of an American Whig
May, 1775

A North Carolina Patriot who wrote extensively in support of the American position, James Iredell nevertheless hoped for reconciliation with Britain until 1776. Following the Declaration of Independence, he helped to draft the laws of the new State of North Carolina. He would be named by President George Washington to serve as an Associate Justice on the first Supreme Court of the United States.

The great Governor of the World, by his supreme and universal Providence, not only conducts the course of nature with unerring wisdom and rectitude, but frequently influences the minds of men to serve the wise and gracious purposes of his providential government; and it is, at all times, our indispensable duty devoutly to acknowledge His superintending Providence, especially in times of impeding danger and public calamity, to reverence and adore His immutable justice as well as to implore His merciful interposition for our deliverance.

> Continental Congress
> Proclamation of a Day of
>   Humiliation, Fasting and Prayer
> (Committee: William Hooper,
>   Robert Treat Paine, John Adams)
> June 12, 1775

During a time of deep concern for the future of the Patriot cause, the Continental Congress urged all the citizens of the American Colonies to turn to prayer.

With united hearts and voices, [we] unfeignedly confess and deplore our many sins; and offer up our joint supplications to the all-wise, omnipotent, and merciful Disposer of all events; humbly beseeching him to forgive our iniquities ... that the divine blessing may descend and rest upon all our civil rulers, and upon the representatives of the people ... that virtue and true religion may revive and flourish throughout our land ... and that her civil and religious privileges may be secured to the latest posterity.

> Continental Congress
> Proclamation of a Day of
>   Humiliation, Fasting and Prayer
> (Committee: William Hooper,
>   Robert Treat Paine, John Adams)
> June 12, 1775

The battles at Concord and Lexington informed the Continental Congress that relations with Britain, the greatest military power in the world, had reached the critical point. The greatest wisdom was now required.

We do then most solemnly before God and the world declare that, regardless of every consequence, at the risk of every distress, we will [exert] to their utmost energies all those powers which our Creator hath given us to preserve that liberty which He committed to us in sacred deposit, and to protect from every hostile hand our lives and our properties.

Thomas Jefferson
Declaration of Continental Congress
    on Taking up Arms (Draft)
June, 1775

The time had come to form the Continental Army, and the Patriots considered themselves obligated to explain their position to the citizens of Britain and the world.

A reverence for our great Creator, principles of humanity, and the dictates of common sense must convince all those who will reflect upon the subject that government was instituted to promote the welfare of mankind, and ought to be administered for the attainment of that end.... We esteem ourselves bound by obligations of respect to the rest of the world, to make known the justice of our cause.

John Dickinson
Declaration of Continental Congress
on Taking up Arms (Draft)
July, 1775

As with every resolution of the Continental Congress, ideas were received from many delegates. Both John Dickinson and Thomas Jefferson contributed their words to this important justification of the American cause.

While we are contending for our own liberty, we should be very cautious of violating the rights of conscience in others, ever considering that God alone is the judge of the hearts of men, and to Him only in this case, they are answerable.

> George Washington
> Letter to Colonel Benedict Arnold
> September 14, 1775

As Colonel Benedict Arnold took charge of an expedition against the British in Catholic Quebec, General George Washington, the new commander-in-chief of the Continental Army, reminded him of a key principle of the American Revolution. Ultimately Arnold would betray the Patriot cause, but Washington would surmount all obstacles in leading the United States to victory.

He who is void of virtuous attachments in private life is, or very soon will be, void of all regard for his country. There is seldom an instance of a man guilty of betraying his country, who had not before lost the feeling of moral obligations in his private connections....

Since private and public vices are in reality, so nearly connected, how necessary is it that the utmost pains be taken by the public to have the principles of virtue early inculcated on the minds of children, and the moral sense kept alive, and that the wise institutions of our ancestors for these great purposes be encouraged by the government. For no people will tamely surrender their liberties, nor can any be easily subdued, when knowledge is diffused and virtue is preserved.

Samuel Adams
Letter to James Warren
November 4, 1775

Although the Revolutionary War had begun, Samuel Adams was less concerned about military strength than the supportive virtue of the people. Anticipating victory for the American cause, he looked ahead to the education of future generations.

We may look up to armies for our defense, but virtue is our best security. It is not possible that any state should long remain free, where virtue is not supremely honored.... The leading gentlemen [would] do eminent service to the public by impressing upon the minds of the people the necessity and importance of encouraging that system of education which is so well calculated to diffuse among the individuals of the community the principles of morality, so necessary to the preservation of public liberty.

> Samuel Adams
> Letter to James Warren
> November 4, 1775

Samuel Adams was clearly one of the most outspoken Patriots of his day. As revealed by the quotations throughout this book, his views concerning the necessity of morality were shared by the other leaders of the American cause.

A true patriot must be a religious man.... He who neglects his duty to his Maker may well be expected to be deficient and insincere in his duty towards the public.

> Abigail Adams
> Letter to John Adams
> November 5, 1775

The writings of American women on the subjects of religion and virtue were seldom saved during the formative years of this nation. Abigail Adams wrote these words to her husband, John, after meeting with Benjamin Franklin in Boston.

The form of government which you admire, when its principles are pure, is admirable indeed. It is productive of everything which is great and excellent among men. But its principles are as easily destroyed as human nature is corrupted. Such a government is only to be supported by pure religion, or austere morals. Public virtue cannot exist in a nation without private [virtue]; and public virtue is the only foundation of republics. There must be a positive passion for the public good, the public interest, honor, power, and glory established in the minds of the people, or there can be no republican government, nor any real liberty.

John Adams
Letter to Mercy Otis Warren
April 16, 1776

Mercy Otis Warren, who would become the only woman of the Revolutionary War period to publish an American history, speculated about the establishment of a democratic republic, similar to the form of government that would be set forth in the Constitution of the United States eleven years later. In his reply to her letter, John Adams outlined the essential requirements for the success of a government directed by the vote of the people.

Revelation assures us that "righteousness exalteth a nation" — Communities are dealt with in this world by the wise and just Ruler of the Universe. He rewards or punishes them according to their general character.... The public liberty will not long survive the extinction of morals.

Samuel Adams
Letter to John Scollay
April 30, 1776

At the time Samuel Adams wrote these words, the majority of the delegates to the Continental Congress were beginning to accept the inevitability of the goal he had supported for so long: independence.

No man has a more perfect reliance on the all-wise and powerful dispensations of the Supreme Being than I have, nor thinks His aid more necessary.

George Washington
Letter to Reverend William Gordon
May 13, 1776

General Washington's faith would soon be tested by Britain's military strength and by lack of resources for the Continental Army. However, he would persevere through the hardships and occasional betrayals of the next seven years until victory and peace were achieved.

No free government, nor the blessings of liberty, can be preserved to any people except by a firm adherence to justice, moderation, temperance, frugality, and virtue.

George Mason
Virginia Declaration of Rights
(First Draft)
May, 1776

George Mason, one of the oldest and most prominent Virginia Patriots, served as a particular inspiration to Thomas Jefferson, who would prepare the Declaration of Independence within a matter of weeks.

Statesmen may plan and speculate for liberty, but it is religion and morality alone which can establish the principles upon which freedom can securely stand. The only foundation of a free Constitution is pure virtue, and if this cannot be inspired into our people ... they may change the forms of government, but they will not obtain a lasting liberty.   They will only exchange tyrants and tyrannies.

John Adams
Letter to Zabdiel Adams
June 21, 1776

The day of decision on the issue of independence was fast approaching. As a member of the Continental Congress, John Adams was committed to the establishment of a new government for America, but in a family letter he revealed his uncertainty about the ability of the people to maintain their liberty.

It may be the will of Heaven that America shall suffer calamities still more wasting and distresses yet more dreadful. If this is to be the case, it will have this good effect, at least: it will inspire us with many virtues, which we have not, and correct many errors, follies, and vices, which threaten to disturb, dishonor, and destroy us. The furnace of affliction produces refinement, in States as well as individuals. And the new governments we are assuming, in every part, will require a purification from our vices, and an augmentation of our virtues or they will be no blessings.... But I must submit all my hopes and fears to an overruling Providence; in which, unfashionable as the faith may be, I firmly believe.

John Adams
Letter to Abigail Adams
July 3, 1776

On July 2, 1776, the Continental Congress had agreed to declare independence from Britain, but the delegates required two more days to clarify wording in the document they would sign. Once the decision was made, John Adams expressed his concerns and hopes to his wife.

We hold these truths to be self-evident, that all men are created equal, that they are endowed by their Creator with certain unalienable rights, that among these are life, liberty, and the pursuit of happiness.

Thomas Jefferson
The Declaration of Independence
    as Adopted by Congress
July 4, 1776

This document effectively summarized the passions, grievances, dreams and concepts of government held by the founders of the new United States of America. The phrase "we hold these truths to be self-evident" was suggested by Benjamin Franklin.

We, therefore, the representatives of the United States of America, in General Congress, assembled, appealing to the Supreme Judge of the world for the rectitude of our intentions, do, in the name, and by authority of the good people of these Colonies, solemnly publish and declare, that these United Colonies are, and of right ought to be free and independent States ... and that as free and independent States, they have full power to levy war, conclude peace, contract alliances, establish commerce, and to do all other acts and things which independent States may of right do. And for the support of this Declaration, with a firm reliance on the protection of divine Providence, we mutually pledge to each other our lives, our fortunes and our sacred honor.

> Thomas Jefferson
> The Declaration of Independence
>   as Adopted by Congress
> July 4, 1776

These words capture the spirit of the American Revolution and the determination of the Patriots to establish a government based on the aspirations of the people.

All government ought to be instituted and supported for the security and protection of the community ... and to enable the individuals who compose it to enjoy their natural rights and the other blessings which the Author of existence has bestowed upon man. We [confess] the goodness of the great Governor of the universe (who alone knows to what degree of earthly happiness mankind may attain, by perfecting the arts of government) in permitting the people by common consent and without violence, deliberately to form for themselves such just rules as they shall think best for governing their society.

Constitution of Pennsylvania
Benjamin Franklin, President
of the Convention
July 15, 1776

During 1776, each of the former Colonies began to establish its own State government, often with an appeal to God.

May God give us wisdom, fortitude, perseverance and every other virtue necessary for us to maintain that independence which we have asserted.

Samuel Adams
Letter to John Adams
September 16, 1776

The most famous cousins in the movement for independence reflected on the struggle that lay ahead.

You say that God Almighty has been pleased to bring us together. You say well. He superintends and governs men and their actions. He now sees us. He judges of the sincerity of our hearts, and will punish those who deceive.

Continental Congress
Message to the Six Nations, Delaware
and Shawanese (Shawnee)
December 7, 1776

The Native Americans soon became allies of the British because they feared more rapid encroachment on their lands as a consequence of independence of the United States.

I wish we were a more religious people. That Heaven may bless you here and hereafter is my most ardent prayer.

Samuel Adams
Letter to Elizabeth Adams
December 9, 1776

When Samuel Adams wrote this letter to his wife, he was confronted with the painful possibility that the Patriot cause might be lost.

It becomes all public bodies, as well as private persons, to reverence the Providence of God, and look up to Him as the supreme disposer of all events and the arbiter of the fate of nations.... It [is] recommended to all the United States ... to implore of Almighty God the forgiveness of the many sins prevailing among all [of us].

Continental Congress
Proclamation of a Day of Fasting
   and Humiliation
(Committee: Richard Henry Lee,
   John Witherspoon,
   Samuel Adams)
December 11, 1776

With the Continental Army in retreat at the onset of winter and the government in confusion, three of the most prominent Patriots joined in composing a message to the American people.

If Heaven punishes communities for their vices, how sore must be the punishment of that community who think the rights of human nature not worth struggling for and patiently submit to tyranny. I will rely upon it that [we] will never incur the curse of Heaven for neglecting to defend [our] liberties. I pray God to increase [our] virtue and to make [us] happy in the full and quiet possession of those liberties that [we] have ever so highly prized.

Samuel Adams
Letter to Elizabeth Adams
December 19, 1776

Although the immediate situation still appeared bleak for the American cause, Samuel Adams continued to hope.

Let us do our duty and victory will be our reward.... Let universal charity, public spirit and private virtue be inculcated, encouraged and practiced ... and when you have done these things, then rely upon the good Providence of Almighty God for success, in full confidence that without His blessing all our efforts will evidently fail.

John Jay
Address of the Representatives
  of the State of New York
  to their Constituents
December 23, 1776

The British occupation of the city of New York was a demoralizing factor as 1776 drew to a close, but the Patriots in New York bravely rallied the people.

Freedom is now in your power. Value the heavenly gift. Remember, if you dare to neglect or despise it, you offer an insult to the Divine Bestower.

John Jay
Address of the Representatives
  of the State of New York
  to their Constituents
December 23, 1776

John Jay, who would become one of the most important promoters of the Constitution of the United States and serve as the first Chief Justice of the United States Supreme Court, helped to keep the spark of hope alive during the British occupation of New York, one of the most distressing periods in the Revolutionary War.

If God hath given us freedom, are we responsible to him for that, as well as other talents?... If the means of defense are in our power and we do not make use of them, what excuse shall we make to our children and our Creator? These are questions of the deepest concern to us all. These are questions which materially affect our happiness, not only in this world but in the world to come.... If ever it is incumbent on the people to know truth and to follow it, it is now.

> John Jay
> Address of the Representatives
>   of the State of New York
>   to their Constituents
> December 23, 1776

Captured American soldiers were starved and frozen in British prison ships in New York harbor while Royal officers enjoyed the comfort of the city. At the same time, the Patriots were struggling to find volunteers to maintain the Continental Army.

The man who is conscientiously doing his duty will ever be protected by that righteous and all powerful Being, and when he has finished his work he will receive an ample reward. I am convinced that it is my duty to oppose to the utmost of my ability the designs of those who would enslave my country; and with God's assistance I am resolved to oppose them till their designs are defeated or I am called to quit the stage of life.

> Samuel Adams
> Letter to Elizabeth Adams
> January 29, 1777

Perhaps cheered by the news of General Washington's capture of Hessian mercenaries employed by the British, Samuel Adams exhibited renewed determination, even in the depth of winter.

God bless you, and grant success to America ... with wisdom and virtue to secure peace and happiness to her sons in all future ages.

Robert Morris
Letter to John Jay
February 4, 1777

Robert Morris, a wealthy Philadelphia merchant, donated and solicited large amounts of money for the Continental Army during early 1777. He would later become the financier of the American Revolution, relying on fellow Philadelphian Haym Salomon to negotiate many complex transactions with foreign buyers of Continental debt.

'Tis a common observation, that our cause is the cause of all mankind, and that we are fighting for their liberty in defending our own.   'Tis a glorious task assigned us by Providence; which has, I trust, given us spirit and virtue equal to it, and will at last crown it with success.

Benjamin Franklin
Letter to Samuel Cooper
May 1, 1777

Although the war had not gone well for the Continental Army during the past year, Benjamin Franklin maintained a sense of optimism based on a belief in the larger purpose of American independence.

What reason is there to expect that Heaven will help those who refuse to help themselves; or that Providence will grant liberty to those who lack courage to defend it? Are the great duties they owe to themselves, their country, and posterity, so soon forgotten?... With firm confidence, trust the event to that Almighty and benevolent Being who hath commanded you to hold fast the liberty with which He has made you free; and who is able as well as willing to support you in performing his orders.

John Jay
Letter to the General Committee
of Tryon County, New York
July 22, 1777

When this letter was written, local Tories and their Native American allies were putting extreme pressure on the Patriots in the Hudson and Mohawk valleys of New York. John Jay's words remain true today.

It is the indispensable duty of all men, to adore the superintending Providence of Almighty God: — To acknowledge with gratitude their obligation to Him for benefits received, and to implore such further blessings as they stand in need of. It [has] pleased Him in his abundant mercy ... to continue to us the innumerable bounties of His common Providence.

Samuel Adams
Draft Resolution for the
Continental Congress
November 1, 1777

Throughout the Revolutionary War, the Continental Congress advised the American people to take time for prayer. Samuel Adams offered his thoughts on the matter to Congress.

It [is] at all times the duty of a people to acknowledge God in all his ways, and more especially to humble themselves before him when evident tokens of his displeasure are manifested; to acknowledge his righteous government; confess, and forsake their evil ways; and implore his mercy.

It is recommended to the United States of America ... at one time, and with one voice, the inhabitants may acknowledge the righteous dispensations of Divine Providence, and confess their iniquities and transgressions, ... implore the mercy and forgiveness of God; and beseech him that vice, profaneness, extortion, and every evil, may be done away; and that we may be a reformed and happy people.

> Continental Congress
> Proclamation of a Day of Fasting,
> Humiliation and Prayer
> (Committee: John Harvie,
> Elbridge Gerry,
> Abraham Clark)
> March 7, 1778

Toward the end of the bitter winter endured by American soldiers at Valley Forge, the Continental Congress again reminded the people to make an appeal to God.

The people in America have now the best opportunity and the greatest trust in their hands, that Providence ever committed to so small a number, since the transgression of the first pair [Adam and Eve]; if they betray their trust, their guilt will merit even greater punishment than other nations have suffered, and the indignation of Heaven.

> Continental Congress
> A Defense of the Constitutions of
>   Government of the United States
>   of America
> (Prepared by John Adams)
> March 22, 1778

After the winter of British occupation of Philadelphia, the Continental Congress addressed the American people in an effort to reinvigorate the Patriot cause.

Let us compare every constitution we have seen with those of the United States of America, and we shall have no reason to blush for our country. On the contrary, we shall feel the strongest motives to fall upon our knees in gratitude to Heaven for having been graciously pleased to give us birth and education in this country, and for having destined us to live under her laws!

> Continental Congress
> A Defense of the Constitutions of
>   Government of the United States
>   of America
> (Prepared by John Adams)
> March 22, 1778

The arrival of military and financial aid from France during 1778 would soon strengthen both the Continental Army and the Continental Congress.

Review the great scenes of history: you will find mankind have always been obliged to pay dear for the blessings they enjoyed.... The struggles of a great people have almost always ended in the establishment of liberty.... Such a people are spoken of with admiration by all future ages....

Their souls glow with gratitude for the virtue and self-denial of their forefathers. They consider them as patterns for their own conduct on similar occasions and are continually pointing them out to the reverence and imitation of their children. These are the glorious effects of patriotism and virtue. These are the rewards annexed to the faithful discharge of that great and honorable duty, fidelity to our country.... I pray to God that the fair character I have described may be that of America to the latest ages.

James Iredell
Charge to the Grand Jury
    at Edenton, North Carolina
May 1, 1778

James Iredell, an important spokesman for the Patriot cause in North Carolina, would be appointed to the first Supreme Court of the United States in 1789. In 1778, as a Superior Court Judge under the new government of North Carolina, which he helped to form, he explained his view of the principles of the Revolutionary War to a jury in his home community.

While we are zealously performing the duties of good citizens and soldiers we certainly ought not to be inattentive to the higher duties of religion. To the distinguished character of patriot, it should be our highest glory to add the more distinguished character of Christian. The signal instances of providential goodness which we have experienced and which have now almost crowned our labors with complete success, demand from us the warmest returns of gratitude and piety to the Supreme Author of all Good.

George Washington
Orders to the Continental Army
May 2, 1778

General Washington emerged form the Valley Forge experience with renewed determination, but final military success in the Revolutionary War would be more than three years away.

The religion of America is the religion of all mankind. Any person may worship in the manner he thinks most agreeable to the Deity; and if he behaves as a good citizen, no one concerns himself as to his faith or adorations, neither have we the least solicitude to exalt any one sect or profession above another.

Samuel Adams
Letter from "An American"
    to the Earl of Carlisle and others
July 16, 1778

Samuel Adams had been the driving force in maintaining the Patriot spirit in New England during the early 1770s because he reflected the beliefs of the people. He continued to promote the American cause in his writing during the Revolutionary War even as the Continental Army was beginning to gain greater respect on the battlefield.

The hand of Providence has been so conspicuous in all this, that he must be worse than an infidel who lacks faith, and more than wicked who has not gratitude enough to acknowledge his obligations.

George Washington
Letter to Brigadier General
Thomas Nelson
August 20, 1778

Reflecting on the fact that the American forces and their British adversaries had regrouped in much the same position as they had found themselves two years earlier — and that a fleet of French ships had arrived to assist the American cause — General George Washington ascribed the Continental Army's ability to continue the Revolutionary War to a primary source: assistance from God.

True religion and good morals are the only solid foundations of public liberty and happiness.

Continental Congress
Resolution
October 12, 1778

In the midst of the Revolutionary War, the Continental Congress reminded the American people of the underlying principle of the Patriot cause.

Public liberty will not long survive the loss of public virtue.

> Samuel Adams
> Letter to Samuel Cooper
> December 25, 1778

The official views of the Continental Congress expressed in its resolutions, such as that quoted on the previous page, were supported privately by the members, among them Samuel Adams.

When I consider the settlement of this country ... and the magnanimity, fortitude and perseverance with which the militia ... vindicated their liberty, with superior lustre in arms, freedom of constitution and government; and above all, in the righteousness of their cause, I cannot reflect on the mighty scene without amazement, and acknowledging the propitious agency of Deity.

Ethan Allen
Letter to the Inhabitants of Vermont
January 9, 1779

Ethan Allen was the leader of the "Green Mountain Boys" of Vermont and the officer who seized control of Fort Ticonderoga from the British — declaring that he did so by the authority of "the Great Jehovah and the Continental Congress." Although a self-proclaimed Deist, he referred to "righteousness" and "propitious agency" in his Letter to the Inhabitants of Vermont.

Notwithstanding the chastisements received and benefits bestowed, too few of us have been sufficiently awakened to a sense of their guilt, or warmed with gratitude, or taught to amend their lives and turn from their sins, that so He might turn from His wrath.

Resolved, that it be recommended to the several States to appoint ... a day of fasting, humiliation and prayer to Almighty God, that He will be pleased to avert those impeding calamities which we have too well deserved: that He will grant us his grace to repent of our sins, and amend our lives, according to his holy word: that He will continue that wonderful protection which hath led us through the paths of danger and distress: that He will be a husband to the widow and a father to the fatherless children ... that He will grant us patience in suffering, and fortitude in adversity; that He will inspire us with humility and moderation, and gratitude in prosperous circumstances ... that He will diffuse useful knowledge, extend the influence of true religion, and give us that peace of mind, which the world cannot give; that He will be our shield in the day of battle, our comforter in the hour of death, and our kind parent and merciful judge through time and through eternity.

> Continental Congress
> Proclamation of a Day of Fasting,
>   Humiliation and Prayer
> (Committee: Gouverneur Morris,
>   William Henry Drayton,
>   William Paca)
> March 20, 1779

This is a rare expression of religious views by Gouverneur Morris. He would play a key role in the Constitutional Convention eight years later.

It is with great sincerity I join you in acknowledging and admiring the dispensations of Providence in our favor. America has only to be thankful and to persevere. God will finish his work and establish their freedom.

Benjamin Franklin
Letter to Josiah Quincy
April 22, 1779

The world-famous scientist and elder statesman Benjamin Franklin acknowledged a force greater than military might.

Persevere, and you ensure peace, freedom, safety, glory, sovereignty, and felicity to yourselves, your children, and your children's children. Encouraged by favors already received from infinite goodness, gratefully acknowledging them, earnestly imploring their continuance, constantly endeavoring to draw them down on your heads by an amendment of your lives and a conformity to the Divine will, humbly confiding in the protection so often and wonderfully experienced, vigorously employ the means placed by Providence in your hands for completing your labors....

Diligently promote piety, virtue, brotherly love, learning, frugality, and moderation; and may you be approved before Almighty God worthy of those blessings we devoutly wish you to enjoy.

> Continental Congress
> Message to the Inhabitants of
>   the United States of America
> (Prepared by John Dickinson
>   with William Henry Drayton
>   and James Duane)
> May 26, 1779

As the American people were beginning to tire of the Revolutionary War and the disruption of their lives, the members of the Continental Congress could see a real possibility that Britain would abandon the war, resulting in true independence for the United States.

Almighty God hath created the mind free, and manifested His supreme will that free it shall remain.... All attempts to influence it by temporal punishments ... tend only to beget habits of hypocrisy and meanness, and are a departure from the plan of the holy author of our religion, who [is] lord both of body and mind.

Thomas Jefferson
A Bill for Establishing Religious
Freedom in Virginia (Draft)
1779

From his early public service until his retirement as the "Sage of Monticello" many years after this resolution was written, Thomas Jefferson worked to assure that all citizens would have the opportunity to worship God in the manner that each individual considered appropriate — without interference by government or by a dominating sect or denomination. Although Jefferson once stated that he had prepared a draft of this important document in 1777, there is no record of its introduction in the Virginia Legislature until 1779. It was finally passed by the General Assembly in 1786.

Heavenly Father, may all revere thee and become thy dutiful children and faithful subjects. May thy laws be obeyed on earth as perfectly as they are in Heaven. Provide for us this day as thou has hitherto daily done. Forgive us our trespasses and enable us likewise to forgive those that offend us. Keep us out of temptation, and deliver us from evil.

> Benjamin Franklin
> "The Lord's Prayer"
> (Personal Papers)
> 1779

In his seventies, Benjamin Franklin continued to study the Bible regularly and meditate on a daily basis. He wrote this interpretation of "the Lord's Prayer" as his personal study guide.

It is the right as well as the duty of all men in society, publicly and at stated seasons, to worship the Supreme Being, the great Creator and Preserver of the universe....

The happiness of a people and the good order and preservation of civil government essentially depend upon piety, religion, and morality, and these cannot be generally diffused through a community except by the institution of the public worship of God and of public instructions in piety, religion, and morality.

> Massachusetts Constitution
> (Drafted by John Adams)
> March 2, 1780

The founders of this nation considered the worship of God as an obligation as well as a privilege, and most of the State constitutions made specific reference to that belief. Because of regional differences in religious preference and the manner of expression, the Constitution of the United States contains no direct reference to God.

It becomes us to endeavor, by humbling ourselves before God, and turning from every evil way, to avert his anger and obtain his favour and blessing. It is therefore recommended ... to implore the sovereign Lord of Heaven and Earth to remember mercy in his judgements; to make us sincerely penitent for our transgressions; to prepare us for deliverance, and to remove the evils with which he hath [visited] us; to banish vice and irreligion from among us, and establish virtue and piety by his divine grace ... to bless all schools and seminaries of learning, and every means of instruction and education; to cause wars to cease, and to establish peace among the nations.

> Continental Congress
> Proclamation of a Day of Fasting,
>   Humiliation and Prayer
> (Committee: Robert R. Livingston,
>   Roger Sherman, Thomas McKean,
>   William Churchill Houston,
>   James Lovell)
> March 11, 1780

This message was written at the close of another extremely difficult winter for the Continental Army, encamped at Morristown, New Jersey while the British continued to hold New York. The year 1780 would present many new challenges, as well as hopeful signs, for the American leaders.

The people of this country properly considered themselves as called by God, and warranted by Him, to encounter every hazard in the common cause of man. Be assured, my dear countrymen, the liberty, the happiness of America, and its consequence in the eyes of the world, depend upon our present activity and spirit.

Samuel Adams
Letter to *The Boston Gazette*
June 12, 1780

The words of Samuel Adams, backed up by his long years of service to the American cause, had helped to rally the Patriots of Massachusetts for many years. Despite ongoing difficulties faced by the Continental Army, his optimistic phrases began to appear more realistic as the summer of 1780 progressed.

If you carefully fulfill the various duties of life, from a principle of obedience to your heavenly Father, you shall enjoy that peace which the world cannot give nor take away.

Samuel Adams
Letter to Hannah Adams
August 17, 1780

The beliefs of our nation's founders, as revealed in their letters to family and friends, are consistent with their public advice and prayers.

I congratulate you and my country on the singular favor of heaven in the peaceable and auspicious settlement of our government upon a Constitution formed by wisdom, and sanctified by the solemn choice of the people who are to live under it. May the Supreme Ruler of the world be pleased to establish and perpetuate these new foundations of liberty and glory.

John Hancock
Inaugural Address as Governor
of Massachusetts
October 25, 1780

Best known for his bold signature on the Declaration of Independence as the President of the Continental Congress, John Hancock was for many years thereafter Governor of Massachusetts.

Sensible of the importance of Christian piety and virtue to the order and happiness of a state, I earnestly commend to you every measure for their support and encouragement that shall not infringe the rights of conscience, which I rejoice to see established by the Constitution on so broad a basis; and if anything can be further done on the same basis for the relief of the public teachers of religion and morality, an order of men greatly useful to their country ... I shall most readily concur with you in every such measure.

John Hancock
Inaugural Address as Governor
  of Massachusetts
October 25, 1780

John Hancock's words represented the opinion of the people of Massachusetts. In fact, his fellow Patriot and political rival, Samuel Adams (President of the State Senate and later Governor himself) was far more outspoken on these matters.

A due observation of the Lord's Day is not only important to internal religion, but greatly conductive to the order and benefit of civil society. It speaks to the senses of mankind, and, by a solemn cessation from their common affairs, reminds them of a deity and their accountableness to the great Lord of all.

John Hancock
Inaugural Address as Governor
   of Massachusetts
October 25, 1780

One of the most obviously wealthy men in the United States, John Hancock was also the most popular politician in Massachusetts. Through his early involvement in the Patriot cause and his key role in the Continental Congress, combined with his authoritative appearance, he had become a symbol of the new State government.

Manners — by which not only the freedom, but the very existence of republics, are greatly affected — depend much upon the public institutions of religion and the good education of youth; in both these instances our fathers laid a wise foundation, for which their posterity have had reason to bless their memory. The public schools ... very early founded by them, have been no small support to the cause of liberty, and given no dishonorable distinction to our country. The advantages they are still capable of affording to the present and future generations are unspeakable. I cannot, therefore, omit warmly to commend them to your care and patronage.... May Heaven assist us to set out well.

> John Hancock
> Inaugural Address as Governor
>   of Massachusetts
> October 25, 1780

John Hancock, who would serve as Governor of Massachusetts (except for one term in Congress) until his death in 1793, set forth the principles of the American Revolution in his first inaugural address.

I believe that a wise and good Being governs this world, that he has ordered us to travel through it to a better one, and that we have nothing but our duty to do on the journey, which will not be a long one. Let us therefore travel on with spirits and cheerfulness, without grumbling.... Let us enjoy prosperity when we have it, and in adversity endeavor to be patient and resigned, without being lazy or insensible.

John Jay
Letter to Silas Deane
November 1, 1780

At this time, John Jay served as representative of the Continental Congress to the Spanish government. While there, he worked to obtain support for the United States and awaited news of the latest campaign by the Continental Army, now engaged in the fifth year of war.

If men of wisdom and knowledge, of moderation and temperance, of patience, fortitude and perseverance, of sobriety and true republican simplicity of manners, of zeal for the honor of the Supreme Being and the welfare of the common wealth — if men possessed of these and other excellent qualities are chosen to fill the seats of government, we may expect that our affairs will rest on a solid and permanent foundation.

> Samuel Adams
> Letter to Elbridge Gerry
> November 27, 1780

In correspondence between two former Massachusetts delegates to the Continental Congress, the link between virtue and successful government by the people is emphasized once again.

At all times it is our duty to acknowledge the over-ruling providence of the great Governor of the universe, and devoutly to implore his divine favor and protection ... that we may, with united hearts, confess and bewail our manifold sins and transgressions, and by sincere repentance and amendment of life, appease his righteous displeasure, and through the merits of our blessed Saviour, obtain pardon and forgiveness: that it may please Him to inspire all our citizens with a fervent and unselfish love of their country, and to preserve and strengthen their union ... that the blessings of peace and liberty may be established on an honorable and permanent basis, and transmitted inviolate to the latest posterity: that it may please Him ... to bless us with health and plenty: that it may please Him to bless all schools and seminaries of learning, and to grant that truth, justice and benevolence, and pure and undefiled religion, may universally prevail.

> Continental Congress
> Proclamation of a Day of
>   Humiliation, Fasting and Prayer
> (Committee: James Duane,
>   Jesse Root, James Madison)
> March 20, 1781

Sensing that the year 1781 would be crucial to the success of the Patriot cause, the Continental Congress urged the American people to renew their trust in God.

Let each citizen remember, at the moment he is offering his vote, that he is not making a present or a compliment to please an individual, or at least that he ought not so to do; but that he is executing one of the most solemn trusts in human society, for which he is accountable to God and his country.

Samuel Adams
Letter to *The Boston Gazette*
April 2, 1781

During the first election under the new Massachusetts Constitution, Samuel Adams offered his advice to the voters.

Whereas it hath pleased Almighty God, father of mercies, remarkably to assist and support the United States of America in their important struggle for liberty ... it is the duty of all to observe and thankfully acknowledge the interpositions of his Providence in their behalf....

It is recommended ... that all the people may assemble ... with grateful hearts, to celebrate the praises of our gracious Benefactor; to confess our manifold sins; offer up our most fervent supplications to the God of all grace, that it may please Him to pardon our offences, and incline our hearts for the future to keep all his laws; to comfort and relieve all our brethren who are in distress or captivity ... to bless all seminaries of learning; and cause the knowledge of God to cover the earth, as the waters cover the seas.

> Continental Congress
> Proclamation of a Day of
>   Thanksgiving and Prayer
> (Committee: John Witherspoon,
>   Joseph Montgomery,
>   James Mitchell Varnum,
>   Roger Sherman)
> October 26, 1781

Following the surrender of the main British force at Yorktown, Virginia, the members of the Continental Congress had reason to believe that independence was at hand. They asked the American people to give thanks to God.

Can the liberties of a nation be thought secure when we have removed their only firm basis, a conviction in the minds of the people that these liberties are of the gift of God? That they are not to be violated but with his wrath? Indeed I tremble for my country when I reflect that God is just; that his justice cannot sleep forever.

Thomas Jefferson
Notes on Virginia, Query XVIII
1781

At the time that Americans were celebrating their liberation from British rule, Thomas Jefferson expressed his concern about black slavery.

[May] our joint supplications ascend to the throne of the Ruler of the Universe beseeching Him to diffuse a spirit of universal reformation among all ranks and degrees of our citizens; and make us a holy, that so we may be an happy people; that it would please Him to impart wisdom, integrity and unanimity to our counsellors ... establish peace in all our borders, and give happiness to all our inhabitants ... that He would incline the hearts of all men to peace, and fill them with universal charity and benevolence.

> Continental Congress
> Proclamation of a Day of Fasting,
>   Humiliation and Prayer
> (Committee: Joseph Montgomery,
>   Oliver Wilcott, John Morin Scott)
> March 19, 1782

When military victory had been achieved, the leaders of the United States did not forget God. Quite the contrary: they turned to prayer.

I cannot part with the comfortable belief of a Divine Providence; and the more I see the impossibility of giving equivalent punishment to a wicked man in this life, the more I am convinced of a future state, in which all that here appears to be wrong shall be set right, all that is crooked made straight.

Benjamin Franklin
Letter to James Hutton
July 7, 1782

At age 76, Benjamin Franklin continued his lifelong inquiry concerning the activities of men and the judgment of God.

Industry and constant employment are great preservatives of the morals and virtue of a nation.... And the Divine Being seems to have manifested his approbation of the mutual forbearance and kindness with which the different sects treat each other, by the remarkable prosperity with which He has been pleased to favor the whole country.

Benjamin Franklin
Information to Those Who Would Remove to America
September, 1782

Throughout his life, Benjamin Franklin expressed his belief in a relationship between God and the actions of the American people that can be witnessed in history.

It being the indispensable duty of all nations, not only to offer up their supplications to Almighty God, the giver of all good, for His gracious assistance in a time of distress, but also in a solemn and public manner to give Him praise for His goodness in general, and especially for great and signal interpositions of His Providence in their behalf; therefore, the United States in Congress assembled, taking into consideration the many instances of divine goodness to these States ... recommend to the inhabitants ... to testify their gratitude to God for his goodness, by a cheerful obedience to His laws, and by promoting, each in his station, and by his influence, the practice of true and undefiled religion, which is the great foundation of public prosperity and national happiness.

> Continental Congress
> Proclamation of a Day
>   of Thanksgiving
> (Committee: Joseph Montgomery,
>   Hugh Williamson,
>   John Witherspoon)
> October 11, 1782

While awaiting word from the peace negotiations in Europe, members of the Continental Congress called for Thanksgiving by the American people. Our nation's founders continuously pointed out the link between religion and national happiness.

If you make good use of and continue improving those abilities and that knowledge you now possess, your usefulness in this life under God may be of some importance to your fellow creatures....

Without the almighty power of the Spirit of God, enlightening your mind, subduing your will, and continually drawing you to himself — you can do nothing.

Be not afraid to go to him as your Father — your Friend and your God.... To Him be Glory forever.

Elias Boudinot
Letter to Susan Boudinot
October 30, 1782

The public statements on spirituality by American leaders rested on the same foundation as the private views of the less well known citizens who played important roles in establishing the government of the United States. Elias Boudinot was one of New Jersey's most active Patriots, serving as "commissary of prisoners" in the Revolutionary War, a delegate to the Continental Congress, Secretary of Foreign Affairs, and a member of the House of Representatives for the first six years under the Constitution, which he helped to ratify in the New Jersey convention. He was named President of the Continental Congress one week after this letter was written to his daughter.

Let it be remembered, finally, that it has ever been the pride and boast of America that the rights for which she contended were the rights of human nature. By the blessing of the Author of these rights on the means exerted for their defense, they have prevailed against all opposition. If justice, good faith, honor, gratitude, and all the other qualities which ennoble the character of a nation and fulfill the ends of government, be the fruit of our establishments, the cause of liberty will acquire a dignity and luster which it has never yet enjoyed; and an example will be set which cannot but have the most favorable influence on the rights of mankind.

> Continental Congress
> Address to the Thirteen States
> (Prepared by James Madison,
>   assisted by committee members
>   Oliver Ellsworth and
>   Alexander Hamilton)
> April 26, 1783

The Continental Congress, which had recently developed a plan for beginning to repay the public debt incurred during the Revolutionary War, called upon James Madison to communicate their views to the governments and citizens of the States.

I now make it my earnest prayer that God would have you in His holy protection, that He would incline the hearts of the citizens to cultivate a spirit of subordination and obedience to government, to entertain a brotherly affection and love for one another, for their fellow citizens of the United States at large, and particularly for their brethren who have served in the field, and finally, that He would most graciously be pleased to dispose us all, to do justice, to love mercy, and to demean ourselves with that charity, humility and pacific temper of mind, which were the characteristics of the divine Author of our blessed religion, and without an humble imitation of whose example in these things, we can never hope to be a happy nation.

George Washington
Circular Letter to the States
June 8, 1783

Before resigning his commission as Commander-in-Chief of the Continental Army, George Washington sent a lengthy message to the Governors of the thirteen State governments, urging them to form "an indissoluble Union of the States under one Federal head."

In the midst of our joys, I hope we shall not forget that to divine Providence is to be ascribed the glory and the praise.

George Washington
Letter to Reverend John Rodgers
June 11, 1783

As he prepared to leave the Continental Army, George Washington looked beyond the military victories that had brought about the recent peace agreement and the true independence of the United States.

Liberty! Thou emanation from the all-beauteous and celestial mind! To Americans thou hast committed the guardianship of the darling rights of mankind.... Inspired by the virtuous [States], who are now the pride and will be ever the boast of America, they will instill this holy truth into the infant minds of their children, and teach them to hold it sacred, even as the divine aphorisms of religion, that the safety of America will be found in her Union.

James Madison
"The North American," No. II
October 8, 1783

These words, from a newspaper essay attributed to James Madison, were evidently written while most members of the Continental Congress had vacated Philadelphia in order to avoid a confrontation with unpaid American soldiers. Although favoring a limitation on the power of the central government, Madison argued that the Articles of Confederation were insufficient and that a stronger union of the States was required.

The interposition of Divine Providence in our favor has been most abundantly and most graciously manifested, and the citizens of these United States have every reason for praise and gratitude to the God of their salvation. Impressed, therefore, with an exalted sense of the blessings by which we are surrounded, and of our entire dependence on that Almighty Being, from whose goodness and bounty they are derived ... all the people may assemble to celebrate with grateful hearts and united voices, the praises of their Supreme and all bountiful Benefactor, for His numberless favors and mercies.

> Continental Congress
> Proclamation of a Day
>   of Thanksgiving
> (Committee: James Duane,
>   Samuel Huntington,
>   Samuel Holten)
> October 18, 1783

Now that a peace agreement was at hand, the delegates to the Continental Congress renewed their call for prayer and thanksgiving.

Disposed, at every suitable opportunity to acknowledge publicly our infinite obligations to the Supreme Ruler of the Universe for rescuing our country from the brink of destruction; I cannot fail at this time to ascribe all the honor of our successes to the same glorious Being....

The establishment of civil and religious liberty was the motive which induced me to the field; the object is attained, and it now remains my earnest wish and prayer that the citizens of the United States would make a wise and virtuous use of the blessings placed before them.

> George Washington
> Address to the Reformed German
>   Congregation of New York
> November 27, 1783

In this address delivered less than one month after his resignation from the Continental Army, George Washington once again emphasized the religious aspect of the American Revolution.

For the confirmation of our independence, for the protection of virtue, philosophy and literature, for the present flourishing state of the sciences, and for the enlarged prospect of human happiness, it is our common duty to pay the tribute of gratitude to the greatest and best of Beings.

George Washington
Address to the Learned Professions
    of Philadelphia
December 13, 1783

Now a private citizen after eight years as Commander-in-Chief of the Continental Army, George Washington was invited to share his advice with organizations throughout the United States.

Thank God, my country is saved and by the smile of Heaven I am a free and independent man.

> John Hancock
> Letter to Captain James Scott
> 1783 [?]

John Hancock expressed the feelings of the people of the United States upon learning that a peace agreement had been reached — eight years after he and Samuel Adams had fled from British troops near Boston.

The citizens of the United States have the greatest reason to return their most hearty and sincere praises and thanksgiving to the God of their deliverance; whose name be praised. Deeply impressed therefore with the sense of the mercies manifested to these United States, and of the blessings which it hath pleased God to shower down on us, of our future dependance, at all times, on his power and mercy as the only source from which so great benefits can be derived; we ... do earnestly recommend ... that all the people of the United States assemble in their respective churches and congregations, to celebrate with grateful hearts, and joyful and united voices, the mercies and praises of their all-bountiful Creator, most holy, and most righteous! for his innumerable favors and mercies vouchsafed unto them.

Continental Congress
A Proclamation of a Day of Prayer
    and Thanksgiving (Draft)
(Committee: Jacob Read,
    Francis Dana, Edward Hand)
August 3, 1784

Operating under the Articles of Confederation, the Continental Congress became increasingly powerless to address the critical issues facing the United States. Attendance declined to the point that there were insufficient votes to pass a thanksgiving proclamation.

While our hearts overflow with gratitude, and our lips pronounce the praises of our great and merciful Creator, we offer up our joint and fervent supplications, that it may please Him of his infinite goodness and mercy, to pardon all our sins and offences; to inspire with wisdom and a true sense of public good, all our public councils; to strengthen and cement the bonds of love and affection between all our citizens; to impress them with an earnest regard for the public good and national faith and honor, and to teach them to improve the days of peace by every good work ... to bless all mankind, and inspire the princes and nations of the earth with the love of peace, that the sound of war may be heard of no more; that He may be pleased to smile upon us ... and to raise up from among our youth, men eminent for virtue, learning and piety, to His service in church and state; to cause virtue and true religion to flourish, to give to all nations amity, peace and concord, and to fill the world with His glory.

> Continental Congress
> Proclamation of A Day of Prayer
>   and Thanksgiving (Draft)
> (Committee: Jacob Read,
>   Francis Dana, Edward Hand)
> August 3, 1784

By the summer of 1784, only nine of the United States were sending delegates to the Continental Congress. Therefore, every resolution required unanimous consent, and even the thanksgiving proclamation was postponed.

If it had not been for the justice of our cause, and the consequent interposition of Providence, in which we had faith, we must have been ruined. If I had ever before been an atheist, I should now have been convinced of the being and government of a Deity! It is He who abases the proud and favors the humble. May we never forget his goodness to us, and may our future conduct manifest our gratitude.

> Benjamin Franklin
> Letter to William Strahan
> August 19, 1784

In his late 70s, Benjamin Franklin saw a religious significance in the success of the American Revolution.

Refiners may weave as fine a web of reason as they please, but the experience of all times shows religion to be the guardian of morals.

Richard Henry Lee
Letter to James Madison
November 26, 1784

Richard Henry Lee, who had introduced the motion in the Continental Congress to declare American independence eight years previously, urged James Madison to reconsider his opposition to a government "assessment" to support churches in Virginia. Ultimately, Madison's interpretation of the Virginia Declaration of Rights prevailed and the plan to use public funds for church support was defeated. When this letter was written, Lee had recently resigned from the Virginia Legislature to attend the Continental Congress.

The strength of a republic is consolidated by its virtues, and righteousness will exalt a nation....

If the leading men in the United States would by precept and example disseminate to the people the principles of piety to God, love to our country and universal benevolence, [we would] secure the favor of Heaven and the honor and esteem of the wise and virtuous part of the world.

> Samuel Adams
> Letter to Richard Henry Lee
> December 23, 1784

Two early spokesmen for American independence, Samuel Adams of Massachusetts and Richard Henry Lee of Virginia, had worked together in the Continental Congress ten years earlier. At this time Adams was President of the Massachusetts Senate, while Lee served as President of the Continental Congress. They continued to exchange ideas for the rest of their lives.

Our political independence does not free us for a moment, either in time or in eternity, from the dependence and the duties which we owe to God, our Redeemer, our neighbors, and ourselves.

Rev. Henry Melchior Muhlenberg
Diary
February 12, 1785

Henry Melchior Muhlenberg was the father of two prominent Patriots — one a General in the Revolutionary War and another who served as the first Speaker of the House of Representatives. Regarded as the founder of the Lutheran church in America, Reverend Muhlenberg was well acquainted with many of the early leaders of our nation.

It is the duty of every man to render to the Creator such homage, and such only, as he believes to be acceptable to Him.... Before any man can be considered as a member of civil society, he must be considered as a subject of the Governor of the Universe.

James Madison
Memorial and Remonstrance
  Against Religious Asessments
June, 1785

James Madison, who would soon become the central figure in the development and ratification of the Constitution of the United States, had long been concerned about religious freedom. When the Virginia Legislature was actively considering the support of churches through government taxation, Madison wrote and circulated a "memorial and remonstrance" (discussion and protest) against the proposal. Interestingly, he refers to a "duty of every man" in relation to God.

While we assert for ourselves a freedom to embrace, to profess and to observe the religion which we believe to be of Divine origin, we cannot deny an equal freedom to those whose minds have not yet yielded to the evidence which has convinced us. If this freedom be abused, it is an offence against God, not against man. To God, therefore, not to man, must an account of it be rendered.

James Madison
Memorial and Remonstrance
Against Religious Asessments
June, 1785

In his protest against a proposal that government should provide financial support to churches, James Madison found himself opposing many of Virginia's most popular personalities, including the persuasive Patrick Henry. Ultimately, Madison was successful in convincing the Legislature to reject the plan to distribute public funds to religious bodies. Personally, Madison was a supporter of the Episcopal church.

The cause of liberty, like most other good causes, will have its difficulties, and sometimes its persecutions, to struggle with. It has advanced more rapidly in this than other countries, but all its objects are not yet attained; and I much doubt whether they ever will be, in this or any other terrestrial state....

All that the best men can do is to persevere in doing their duty to their country, and leave the consequences to Him who made it their duty; being neither elated by success, however great, nor discouraged by disappointments, however frequent and mortifying.

> John Jay
> Letter to the Rev. Doctor Price
> September 27, 1785

While serving as Secretary of Foreign Affairs for the Continental Congress two years before the Constitutional Convention, John Jay offered his thoughts on liberty and duty. This letter was written in support of Reverend Price's campaign against slavery in the United States.

How vain are laws without manners. These cannot be expected unless the strictest attention is paid to the education of youth and the inculcation of true love and fear of the Supreme Being.

It is our earnest wish that you would be pleased strongly to recommend the establishment of schools, of attendance at places of public worship, provision for ministers of the Gospel, and observance of the Sabbath.

> John Dickinson
> Draft Letter (as Governor) to
>   Justices of the Supreme Court
>   of Pennsylvania
> 1785

In the mid-1780s, John Dickinson served as the chief executive of Delaware and then of Pennsylvania. When this draft was written, he expressed the prevailing view of his time. Support of ministers and churches was assumed to be an important aspect of American social organization. However, controversy often arose within the States regarding the propriety of using public funds for that purpose.

I shall point out, in a few words, the influence and advantages of learning upon mankind.

It is friendly to religion, inasmuch as it assists in removing prejudice, superstition and fanaticism, in promoting just notions of the Deity, and in enlarging our knowledge of his works.

It is favorable to liberty. Freedom can exist only in the society of knowledge. Without learning men are incapable of knowing their rights, and where learning is confined to a few people, liberty can be neither equal nor universal.

Benjamin Rush
*A Plan for Establishing Public
Schools in Pennsylvania*
1786

As one of the most respected thinkers of his time, Benjamin Rush was a leader in the movement to make education available to all citizens. In 1786, he also published an important essay urging reform of the Articles of Confederation.

The only foundation for a useful education in a republic is to be laid in religion. Without this there can be no virtue, and without virtue there can be no liberty; and liberty is the object and life of all republican governments.

Benjamin Rush
*A Plan for Establishing Public
Schools in Pennsylvania*
1786

Interestingly, Benjamin Rush was a doctor, a scientist, and a political activist, not a clergyman. As a prominent member of the American Philosophical Society, he continually exchanged ideas with the nation's intellectual leaders, particularly those who were well known for their open inquiry on all subjects.

In this situation — groping, as it were, in the dark to find political truth, and scarce able to distinguish it when presented to us — how has it happened that we have not hitherto once thought of humbly applying to the Father of Lights to illuminate our understandings? ... When we were sensible of danger, we had daily prayers in this room for the Divine Protection. Our prayers, were heard; — and they were graciously answered. All of us ... must have observed frequent instances of a superintending Providence in our favor.... And have we now forgotten that powerful friend? Or do we imagine we no longer need its assistance? I have lived a long time; and the longer I live, the more convincing proofs I see of this truth, that God governs in the affairs of men....

I therefore move that henceforth prayers, imploring the assistance of Heaven and its blessing on our deliberations, be held in this assembly every morning before we proceed to business.

> Benjamin Franklin
> Motion for Prayer in the
>   Constitutional Convention
> June 28, 1787

When the delegates to the Constitutional Convention seemed hopelessly mired in controversy — and dissolution of the United States appeared possible — Benjamin Franklin offered his advice. His motion was tabled in order to avoid possible religious conflicts over the precise wording of prayers at that critical time, but his reminder of the spiritual factor in human relations served to calm passions and introduce a spirit of compromise, which quickly proved successful.

Religion, morality and knowledge being necessary to good government and the happiness of mankind — schools and the means of education shall forever be encouraged.

Continental Congress
An Ordinance for the Government of
   the Territory of the United States
   North West of the River Ohio
July 13, 1787

One of the few lasting actions of the Continental Congress in its final years was passage of the "Northwest Ordinance," which established a procedure for converting the territory north of the Ohio River into member States. The original draft proposal had been prepared by Thomas Jefferson three years earlier.

It is impossible for the man of pious reflection not to perceive in [the ability of the delegates to reach agreement on the Constitution of the United States] a finger of that Almighty Hand, which has been so frequently and signally extended to our relief.

James Madison
The Federalist, No. XXXVII
January 11, 1788

In presenting his highly persuasive case for ratification of the Constitution, James Madison expressed his belief that the new form of government had been developed with Divine assistance.

Our most gracious Creator does not condemn us to sigh for unattainable blessedness; but one thing he demands — that we should seek for happiness in His way, and not in our own.

Humility and benevolence must take place of pride and selfishness. Reason will then discover to us that we cannot be true to ourselves without being true to others — that to love not ourselves only, but our neighbors also, is to love ourselves in the best manner — that to give, is to gain — and ... that we ... correspond with the Divine designs by communicating happiness, as much as we can, to our fellow creatures.

John Dickinson
The Letters of Fabius, Letter I
1788

A series of widely circulated newspaper essays signed "Fabius" helped to build support for the new Constitution of the United States, which required approval of at least nine States before it could become operative among them. The author of the Letters of Fabius was John Dickinson, who had been a delegate to the Constitutional Convention that had prepared the basic document the previous year. He was also a leading spokesman for approval in Delaware, making his State the first to ratify the Constitution.

No one can rejoice more than I do at every step the people of this great country take to preserve the Union, establish good order and government, and to render the nation happy at home and respectable abroad. No country upon earth ever had it more in its power to attain these blessings than United America. Wondrously strange then, and much to be regretted indeed would it be, were we to neglect the means, and to depart from the road which Providence has pointed us, so plainly; I cannot believe it will ever come to pass. The Great Governor of the Universe has led us too long and too far on the road to happiness and glory, to forsake us in the midst of it. By folly and improper conduct, proceeding from a variety of causes, we may now and then get bewildered; but I hope and trust that there is good sense and virtue enough left to recover the right path before we shall be entirely lost.

George Washington
Letter to Benjamin Lincoln
June 29, 1788

When ratification of the Constitution was in doubt, George Washington expressed his concern — and his hope. His words have not lost their significance.

It is our duty, humbly, constantly, fervently, to implore the protection of our most gracious Maker ... and incessantly to strive, as we are commanded, to recommend ourselves to that protection by "doing his will," diligently exercising our reason in fulfilling the purposes for which that [ability] and our existence were given to us....

There is reason to believe that the calamities of nations are the punishments of their sins.

John Dickinson
The Letters of Fabius, Letter VII
1788

Although nine of the United States had ratified the Constitution earlier in the year, New York and Virginia, both vital to the success of the new government, remained undecided. John Dickinson of Delaware continued to urge approval in his "Fabius" essays, which were published as letters in leading newspapers.

I reiterate the professions of my dependence upon Heaven as the source of all public and private blessings. I observe that the general prevalence of piety, philanthropy, honesty, industry, and economy seems, in the ordinary course of human affairs, particularly necessary for advancing and confirming the happiness of our country.... No man who is profligate in his morals, or a bad member of the civil community, can possibly be a true Christian or a credit to his own religious society.

George Washington
Letter to the General Assembly
of Presbyterian Churches
May 26, 1789

During his third month as the first President of the United States, George Washington shared his thoughts on the influence of religion.

The great enemy of the salvation of man, in my opinion, never intended a more effectual means of extirpating Christianity from the world than by persuading mankind that it was improper to read the Bible at schools.

The more I attend to the methods in which education is conducted in our country, the more I am disposed to suspect that our schools and colleges do more harm than good to the interests of humanity, virtue, and religion. What are Latin and Greek and mathematics and philosophy if they do not lead us nearer to the Parent of the Universe and the source and center of all perfection and happiness?

Benjamin Rush
Letter to Jeremy Belknap
July 13, 1789

Although educated primarily in medicine and the sciences, Benjamin Rush continued to express his firm belief that technical knowledge and intellectual concepts do not represent a complete education.

The man must be bad indeed who can look upon the events of the American Revolution without feeling the warmest gratitude towards the great Author of the Universe whose divine interposition was so frequently manifested in our behalf. And it is my earnest prayer that we may so conduct ourselves as to merit a continuance of those blessings with which we have hitherto been favored.

George Washington
Letter to Reverend Samuel Langdon
September 28, 1789

President Washington left little doubt about his belief in the connection between God, proper conduct, and human happiness.

The liberty enjoyed by the people of these States, of worshipping Almighty God agreeably to their consciences, is not only among the choicest of their blessings, but also of their rights. While men perform their social duties faithfully, they do all that society or the state can with propriety demand or expect; and remain responsible only to their Maker for the religion, or modes of faith, which they may prefer or profess.

George Washington
Letter to the Religious Society
of Friends
October, 1789

Like other American leaders of his time, George Washington regarded freedom of religion as the opportunity to worship God without coercion or hindrance, not the exclusion of God from the public consciousness.

It is the duty of all nations to acknowledge the providence of Almighty God, to obey His will, to be grateful for His benefits, and humbly to implore His protection and favor.... Therefore I recommend and assign [a day] to be devoted by the people of these States to the service of that great and glorious Being, who is the beneficent Author of all the good that was, that is, or that will be. That we may all unite in rendering unto Him our sincere and humble thanks, for His kind care and protection of the people of this country previous to their becoming a nation; for the signal and manifold mercies and the favorable interpositions of His providence; for the great degree of tranquillity, union, and plenty, which we have enjoyed; for the peaceable and rational manner in which we have been enabled to establish constitutions of government for our safety and happiness; for the civil and religious liberty with which we are blessed, and the means we have of acquiring and diffusing useful knowledge and in general for all the great and various favors which He hath been pleased to confer upon us.

George Washington
Proclamation of a Day
of Thanksgiving
October 3, 1789

During his first year in office, President Washington introduced the practice ("duty") of issuing an executive proclamation urging nationwide prayer and thanksgiving.

I recommend that we may unite in most humbly offering our prayers and supplications to the great Lord and Ruler of Nations and beseech Him to pardon our national and other transgressions, to enable us all, whether in public or private stations, to perform our duties properly and punctually, to render our national government a blessing to all the people, by constantly being a government of wise, just and constitutional laws, discreetly and faithfully executed and obeyed, to protect and guide all sovereigns and nations (especially such as have shown kindness unto us) and to bless them with good government, peace, and concord. To promote the knowledge and practice of true religion and virtue, and the increase of science among them and us, and generally to grant unto all mankind such a degree of temporal prosperity as He alone knows to be best.

George Washington
Proclamation of a Day
of Thanksgiving
October 3, 1789

Throughout his life, George Washington directed attention to the importance of reverence for God and pursuit of virtue.

I believe in one God, Creator of the universe. That He governs it by his Providence. That He ought to be worshipped. That the most acceptable service we render to Him is doing good to his other children. That the soul of man is immortal, and will be treated with justice in another life respecting its conduct in this.

Benjamin Franklin
Letter to Ezra Stiles
March 9, 1790

Shortly before he died at age 84, Benjamin Franklin summarized his personal beliefs.

Let divines and philosophers, statesmen and patriots impress the minds of men with the importance of educating their boys and girls — of inculcating in the minds of youth the fear and love of Deity, and universal philanthropy; and in subordination to these great principles, the love of their country — of instructing them in the art of self government, without which they never can act a wise part in the government of societies great, or small — in short of leading them in study and practice of the exalted virtues of the Christian system, which will happily tend to subdue the turbulent passions of men and introduce that golden age beautifully described in figurative language: when ... none shall then hurt or destroy, for the Earth shall be full of the knowledge of the Lord.

> Samuel Adams
> Letter to John Adams
> October 4, 1790

While Lieutenant-Governor of Massachusetts, Samuel Adams exchanged ideas with his cousin, the Vice President of the United States.

He who has not a proper regard for men will not have a due reverence for God.

John Dickinson
Miscellaneous Notes (Manuscript)
1790 [?]

Having retired to private life soon after helping to assure ratification of the Constitution, John Dickinson continued to express his views on a variety of subjects. This observation was found among unpublished personal papers.

It should always be remembered that law ... flows from the same divine source: it is the law of God.

Nature, or, to speak more properly, the Author of nature, has done much for us; but it is His gracious appointment and will, that we should also do much for ourselves. What we do, indeed, must be founded on what He has done; and the deficiencies of our laws must be supplied by the perfections of His. Human law must rest its authority, ultimately, upon the authority of that law which is divine.

> James Wilson
> *Lectures on Law: Law and Obligation*
> 1790

One of the foremost lawyers in the United States, James Wilson contributed to the inclusion of an independent judiciary within the Constitution of the United States. (As a delegate to the Constitutional Convention, he wrote the first draft, which was significantly revised before final approval.) He had then taken a major role in persuading the Pennsylvania convention to ratify the new form of government two years before he wrote these words.

That our Creator has a supreme right to prescribe a law for our conduct, and that we are under the most perfect obligation to obey that law, are truths established on the clearest and most solid principles.

James Wilson
Lectures on Law: Law and Obligation
1790

During 1790 and 1791, James Wilson presented a series of addresses, compiled as Lectures on Law, *which explored fundamental legal concepts from an American perspective. At the time, he was the first Professor of Law at the College of Philadelphia (now the University of Pennsylvania) and one of five Associate Justices on the first Supreme Court of the United States.*

How shall we, in particular instances, learn the dictates of our duty, and make, with accuracy, the proper distinction between right and wrong? In other words, how shall we, in particular cases, discover the will of God? We discover it by our conscience, by our reason, and by the Holy Scriptures.

James Wilson
Lectures on Law: Law and Obligation
1790

The leaders of the American Revolution and the Constitutional Convention did not regard the legal system as simply a maze of technicalities, a vehicle for clever maneuvers, or an opportunity for judges to render decisions strictly on the basis of their personal logical capacities. Like James Wilson, they believed that the law was founded on specific religious precepts.

Education accustoms men to thinking and reflection, to reasoning and demonstration. It discovers to them the moral and religious duties they owe to God, their country and to all mankind....

The truly virtuous man, and real patriot, is satisfied with the approbation of the wise and discerning; he rejoices in the contemplation of the purity of his intentions, and waits in humble hope for the plaudit of his final Judge.

Samuel Adams
Letter to John Adams
November 25, 1790

While Samuel Adams was serving the Massachusetts government and John Adams continued to fulfill his undemanding responsibilities as Vice President of the United States, the two Patriot cousins corresponded about other important matters.

The power and goodness of the Almighty were strongly manifested in the events of our glorious revolution, and His kind interposition in our behalf has been no less visible in the establishment of our present equal government. In war He directed the sword and in peace He has ruled in our councils.

George Washington
Letter to the Hebrew Congregations
   of Philadelphia, New York,
   Charleston and Richmond
December 30, 1790

George Washington once again made clear his belief that God plays a vital role in human history.

Whether [the independence of the United States] will prove a blessing or a curse will depend upon the use our people make of the blessings which a gracious God hath bestowed on us. If they are wise, they will be great and happy. If they are of a contrary character, they will be miserable. Righteousness alone can exalt them as a nation.

Reader! whoever thou art, remember this; and in thy sphere, practise virtue thyself, and encourage it in others.

> Patrick Henry
> Personal Papers
> 1790 [?]

This undated statement — which concluded his description of the Stamp Act debates in the Virginia Assembly some twenty-five years earlier — was found among Patrick Henry's personal writings in a sealed envelope with instructions that it should be opened after his death.

We waste so much time and money in punishing crimes, and take so little pains to prevent them. We profess to be republicans, and yet we neglect the only means of establishing and perpetuating our republican forms of government — that is, the universal education of our youth in the principles of Christianity, by means of the Bible; for this divine book, above all others, favors that equality among mankind, that respect for just laws, and all those sober and frugal virtues which constitute the soul of republicanism.

Benjamin Rush
*A Defense of the Use of the Bible
as a School Book*
March 10, 1791

Prominent commentator, political and social activist, and friend of the nation's leaders, Benjamin Rush was deeply concerned about education in the United States. His views were widely shared.

The Bible contains more knowledge necessary to man in his present state than any other book in the world....

If the Bible did not convey a single direction for the attainment of future happiness, it should be read in our schools in preference to all other books, from its containing the greatest portion of that kind of knowledge which is calculated to produce private and public temporal happiness.

Benjamin Rush
*A Defense of the Use of the Bible
as a School Book*
March 10, 1791

Doctor Rush was a respected champion of public education as well as an active participant in the formation of the government of the United States. He was Professor of Medicine at the College of Philadelphia (now the University of Pennsylvania) when this advice was written.

I am sure there never was a people who had more reason to acknowledge a Divine interposition in their affairs than those of the United States; and I should be pained to believe that they have forgotten that agency, which was so often manifested during our revolution, or that they failed to consider the omnipotence of that God who is alone able to protect them.

George Washington
Letter to John Armstrong
March 11, 1792

In the last year of his first term as President, George Washington looked forward to retirement from public office, but he was already under pressure to make himself available for reelection.

As every duty is allied to a blessing, so every right is allied to a duty. There is a relationship that binds mankind together in a system constantly drawing them nearer and nearer to the Divine Author.

> John Dickinson
> "Notes on Government"
> (Manuscript)
> 1792

These unpublished notes were evidently written as background material for the numerous speeches and essays John Dickinson prepared after his retirement from public office.

A virtuous education is calculated to reach and influence the heart, and to prevent crimes.... Such an education, which leads the youth beyond mere outside show, will impress their minds with a profound reverence of the Deity, universal benevolence, and a warm attachment and affection towards their country. It will excite in them a just regard to Divine revelation, which informs them of the original character and dignity of man; and it will inspire them with a sense of true honor, which consists in conforming as much as possible their principles, habits, and manners to that original character.

Samuel Adams
Letter to the Legislature
of Massachusetts
January 17, 1794

Having become Governor of Massachusetts, Samuel Adams conveyed his views on education to the State Legislature.

I feel the impulse of duty strongly, and ... I ought to follow its dictates and commit myself to the care and kindness of that Providence in which we have the highest reason to repose the most absolute confidence....

Let us repose unlimited trust in our Maker; it is our business to adore and to obey.

> John Jay
> Letter to Mrs. Jay
> April 15, 1794

In this letter from Philadelphia (the nation's capital at that time), John Jay, Chief Justice of the Supreme Court, revealed to his wife that "there is here a serious determination to send me to England, if possible to avert a war." He would soon be involved in negotiating a rather weak treaty, which reflected the military unpreparedness of the United States. The agreement was supported by President Washington and ultimately approved by the Senate — and it did provide for the withdrawal of British troops from Michigan and the southern Great Lakes area. Nevertheless, "Jay's Treaty" was violently denounced throughout the country because most Americans, who favored France over Britain in the latest European conflict, wanted the United States to become involved in the war.

The Almighty Author of the Universe has been graciously pleased to place the creatures of mankind [in moral relation to Himself], thus exalting them far above the other inhabitants of the earth. The laws assigned them are rules of action, to be observed.... These include love, reverence, gratitude, trust, and resignation toward their Maker; modesty, purity, and temperance to themselves; and justice, fidelity and benevolence with respect to others.

John Dickinson
The Letters of Fabius, Letter X
(Manuscript)
May 15, 1794

In his retirement, John Dickinson continued to follow the progress and problems of the nation — and to express his views concerning the fundamental principles of the American Revolution.

We call to mind the gracious indulgence of Heaven, by which the American people became a nation, when we survey the general prosperity of our country and look forward to the riches, power, and happiness to which it seems destined....

Let us unite, therefore, in imploring the Supreme Ruler of Nations to spread his holy protection over these United States: ... to perpetuate to our country that prosperity which His goodness has already conferred and to verify the anticipations of this government being a safeguard to human rights.

George Washington
Sixth Annual Address to Congress
November 19, 1794

During the year 1794, two crises faced the second administration of President George Washington: one in foreign relations (British interference with American shipping) and one of domestic origin (an armed rebellion against a Federal tax on the production of whiskey). As ever, he sought divine guidance.

I recommend ... to all persons whomsoever within the United States ... to render their sincere and hearty thanks to the Great Ruler of Nations for the manifold and signal mercies which distinguish our lot as a nation, particularly for the possession of constitutions of government which unite and by their union establish liberty with order; for the preservation of our peace, foreign and domestic, ... and at the same time humbly and fervently to beseech the kind Author of these blessings graciously to prolong them to us; to imprint on our hearts a deep and solemn sense of our obligations to Him for them; to teach us rightly to estimate their immense value; to preserve us from the arrogance of prosperity; ... to dispose us to merit the continuance of His favors by not abusing them, by our gratitude for them, and by [proper] conduct as citizens and men; to render this country more and more a safe and propitious asylum for the unfortunate of other countries; to extend among us true and useful knowledge; to diffuse and establish habits of sobriety, order, morality, and piety; and finally, to impart all the blessings we possess, or ask for ourselves to the whole family of mankind.

George Washington
A Proclamation of a Day
    of Thanksgiving and Prayer
January 1, 1795

Despite the immediate problems he faced, President Washington acknowledged with thanks the many advantages enjoyed by the United States.

Our ancestors, when under the greatest hardships and perils, opened to us the wilderness and left for us an inheritance, one of the best countries under the sun. Amidst their toil and fatigue they extended their views, and early laid the foundation of civil liberty.... They considered morality and real goodness of heart as the great basis upon which the best interests of a nation could be safely laid. Under this idea, they also provided for the institutions of public worship and the support of teachers in piety, religion and morality.... Their perseverance has raised us, by the blessing of Providence, to an exalted degree of prosperity and glory.

> Samuel Adams
> Letter to the Legislature
>   of Massachusetts
> June 3, 1795

As one of the first advocates of American independence, Samuel Adams had done much to further his nation's progress during twenty-five years of public service, but he frequently directed particular attention to the sacrifices of those whose earlier efforts 'ıad paved the way for more recent achievements and benefits, as in this message written while Governor of Massachusetts.

Let us transmit our liberties, our equal rights, our laws and our free republican Constitutions, with their various concomitant blessings, to those who are coming upon the stage of action, and hope in God, that they will be handed down, in purity and energy, to the latest posterity.

Samuel Adams
Letter to the Legislature
of Massachusetts
June 3, 1795

While Samuel Adams gratefully acknowledged the contribution of his forebears, he also emphasized the need to transmit that heritage to future generations.

It appears to me to be the public duty of the people to render unto [our Almighty Sovereign] their sincere and humble thanks, for all His great and unmerited mercies and blessings; and also to offer up to Him their fervent petitions to continue to us His protection and favor: to preserve to us the undisturbed enjoyment of our civil and religious rights and privileges ... — to promote the extension of true religion, virtue and learning — to give us all grace to cultivate national union, concord and good will; and generally to bless our nation, and all other nations, in the manner and measure most conducive to our and their best interests and real welfare.

> John Jay
> Proclamation of Thanksgiving
>   in New York
> November 11, 1795

Having been elected Governor of New York while serving as a special negotiator in Britain for President Washington, John Jay resigned as Chief Justice of the Supreme Court of the United States upon returning home. Near the end of his first year in office, he urged the people of New York to give thanks and seek guidance.

Virtue is the master of all things.... The might of virtue, the power of virtue, is not a very common topic, not as common as it should be.

John Adams
Diary (in *Autobiography*)
August 6, 1796

As other writings of John Adams have shown, his concept of virtue was deeply rooted in religion. In the summer of 1796, he was awaiting the opportunity to become the second President of the United States, an ambition he would soon realize.

I think religion of infinitely higher importance than politics, and I find much cause to reproach myself that I have lived so long and have given no decided and public proofs of my being a Christian. But, indeed, this is a character which I prize far above all this world has or can boast.

Patrick Henry
Letter to Elizabeth Aylett
August 20, 1796

Toward the end of his life, Patrick Henry reflected on his decades of public service in this letter to his daughter. Within the past two years, he had declined two offers by President Washington to serve in the federal government, first a position in the Cabinet and later a seat on the Supreme Court.

Of all the dispositions and habits which lead to political prosperity, religion and morality are indispensable supports.... A volume could not trace all their connections with private and public felicity.... Reason and experience both forbid us to expect that national morality can prevail in exclusion of religious principle.

'Tis substantially true, that virtue or morality is a necessary spring of popular government. The rule indeed extends with more or less force to every species of free government.

George Washington
Farewell Address
September 17, 1796

Before the national election to determine his successor, President George Washington set forth the lessons learned from a lifetime of public service.

Observe good faith and justice towards all nations. Cultivate peace and harmony with all. Religion and morality enjoin this conduct.... Can it be that Providence has not connected the permanent felicity of a nation with its virtue?

George Washington
Farewell Address
September 17, 1796

President Washington undoubtedly hoped that the answer to his question would be obvious.

Whereas it has pleased God, the Father of all Mercies, to bestow upon us innumerable unmerited favors; it highly becomes us duly to recollect His goodness, and in a public and solemn manner to express the grateful feelings of our hearts....

Our civil Constitutions of government, formed by ourselves, and administered by men of our own free election, are by His Grace continued to us. And we still enjoy the inestimable blessings of the Gospel and right of worshipping God according to His own institutions and the honest dictates of our consciences.

Samuel Adams
Proclamation of the Governor
of Massachusetts
October 17, 1796

Throughout his life, Samuel Adams maintained his religious convictions and, as Governor of Massachusetts, continued to share them with the citizens of his State.

Piety, religion and morality have a happy influence on the minds of men, in their public as well as private transactions.... Our children and youth, while they are engaged in the pursuit of useful science, [should] have their minds impressed with a strong sense of the duties they owe to their God, their instructors, and each other, so that when they arrive at a state of manhood, and take a part in any public transactions, their hearts having been deeply impressed in the course of their education with the moral feelings, such feelings may continue and have their due weight through the whole of their future lives.

Samuel Adams
Letter to the Legislature
of Massachusetts
January 27, 1797

Although more outspoken on the subject of religion and education than most political leaders of his time, Samuel Adams represented the views of his constituents. He was elected to public office for much of his working life.

Believing, as I do, that religion and morality are the essential pillars of civil society, I view, with unspeakable pleasure, that harmony and brotherly love which characterizes the clergy of different denominations in the Unites States; exhibiting to the world a new and interesting spectacle, at once the pride of our country and the surest basis of universal harmony.

That your labors for the good of mankind may be crowned with success; that your temporal enjoyments may be commensurate with your merits; and that the future reward of good and faithful servants may be yours, I shall not cease to supplicate the Divine Author of life and felicity.

> George Washington
> Letter to the Clergy
>   in and near Philadelphia
> March 3, 1797

Upon his retirement, former President George Washington bade farewell to the religious leaders in the nation's capital at the time and prayed for their success.

The safety and prosperity of nations ultimately and essentially depend on the protection and blessing of Almighty God; and the national acknowledgment of this truth is not only an indispensable duty, which the people owe to Him, but a duty whose natural influence is favorable to the promotion of that morality and piety, without which social happiness cannot exist, nor the blessings of a free government be enjoyed. This duty, at all times incumbent, is especially so in seasons of difficulty and of danger when existing or threatening calamities, the just judgements of God against prevalent iniquity, are a loud call to repentance and reformation.

John Adams
Proclamation of a Day of Fasting
March 23, 1798

Because President John Adams was concerned that Americans had begun to expect peace and prosperity without effort, he emphasized "repentance and reformation" in his national call for prayer. War with France was becoming a possibility at this time.

I recommend that ... the duties of humiliation and prayer be accompanied by fervent thanksgiving to the Bestower of every good gift, not only for having hitherto protected and preserved the people of these United States in the independent enjoyment of their religious and civil freedom, but also ... for conferring on them many and great favors conducive to the happiness and prosperity of a nation.

John Adams
Proclamation of a Day of Fasting
March 23, 1798

In contrast with today's food fests, fasting was regarded by President Adams as an appropriate means of giving thanks for benefits received.

The great Sovereign of the universe has given us independence, and to that inestimable gift has annexed the duty of defending it.

> John Jay
> Address to the Legislature
>   of New York
> August 2, 1798

Like Governor John Jay, the other founders of this nation saw a close connection between God and civic duty.

We yet humbly and fervently implore the Almighty Disposer of events to avert from our land war and usurpation, the scourges of mankind ... to permit our youth to be educated in virtue ... to maintain the Constitution; and to bless our nation with tranquility, under whose benign influence we may reach the summit of happiness and glory, to which we are destined by nature and nature's God.

James Madison
Address of the General Assembly to
    the People of the Commonwealth
    of Virginia
January 23, 1799

A decade after helping to assure the separation of church and state in the First Amendment to the Constitution of the United States, James Madison wrote this public prayer on behalf of the General Assembly of Virginia. Two years later he would be appointed Secretary of State by President Thomas Jefferson and in 1809 would become the fourth President of the United States.

No truth is more clearly taught in the volume of inspiration, nor any more fully demonstrated by the experience of all ages, than [this]: a deep sense and a due acknowledgement of the governing providence of a Supreme Being — and of the accountableness of men to Him as the searcher of hearts and righteous distributor of rewards and punishments — are conducive to the happiness and rectitude of individuals, and to the well-being of communities.

John Adams
Proclamation of a Day of Fasting
March 6, 1799

Twenty-five years after travelling from Boston to Philadelphia to serve in the first Continental Congress, John Adams maintained his belief that reverence for God is the basis of successful government.

I recommend that the citizens ... devote the time to the sacred duties of religion, in public and in private ... call to mind our numerous offences against the most high God, confess them before Him with the sincerest penitence, implore his pardoning mercy through the Great Mediator and Redeemer for our past transgressions; that through the grace of his Holy Spirit we may be disposed and enabled to yield a more suitable obedience to his righteous requisitions in time to come ... that He would make us deeply sensible that "righteousness exalteth a nation, but that sin is the reproach of any people" ... that He would smile on our colleges, academies, schools, and seminaries of learning, and make them [centers] of sound science, morals, and religion ... and that He would extend the blessings of knowledge, of true liberty, and of pure and undefiled religion throughout the world.

John Adams
Proclamation of a Day of Fasting
March 6, 1799

Again, President John Adams called upon Americans to practice humility in recognition of the benefits they had received.

It would be unbecoming the representatives of this nation to assemble for the first time in this solemn temple [the Capitol of the United States] without looking up to the Supreme Ruler of the Universe and imploring His blessing.

May this territory be the residence of virtue and happiness! In this city may that piety and virtue, that wisdom and magnanimity, that constancy and self-government, which adorned the great character whose name it bears be forever held in veneration! Here and throughout our country may simple manners, pure morals, and true religion flourish forever!

John Adams
Fourth Annual Address to Congress
November 22, 1800

President John Adams expressed his hope for the future of American government. Its center of operations had recently been moved from Philadelphia to the new city of Washington in the District of Columbia.

Enlightened by a benign religion, professed indeed and practiced in various forms, yet all of them including honesty, truth, temperance, gratitude, and the love of man; acknowledging and adoring an overruling Providence, which by all its dispensations proves that it delights in the happiness of man here and his greater happiness hereafter; with all these blessings, what more is necessary to make us a happy and prosperous people? Still one thing more, fellow citizens — a wise and frugal government.

Thomas Jefferson
First Inaugural Address
March 4, 1801

President Thomas Jefferson, who had defeated the incumbent John Adams, was more reserved in his statements concerning religion — but he did not exclude the issue from public life.

When we ... consider the state of our beloved country, our just attentions are first drawn to those pleasing circumstances which mark the goodness of that Being from whose favor they flow and the large measure of thankfulness we owe for His bounty. Another year has come around and finds us still blessed with peace and friendship abroad [and] law, order and religion at home.

Thomas Jefferson
Second Annual Message to Congress
December 15, 1802

President Thomas Jefferson's domestic priorities are noteworthy.

I shall need the favor of that Being in whose hands we are, who led our fathers, as Israel of old, from their native land and planted them in a country flowing with all the necessaries and comforts of life; who has covered our infancy with His providence and our riper years with His wisdom and power, and to whose goodness I ask you to join in supplications with me that He will so enlighten the minds of your servants, guide their councils, and prosper their measures that whatsoever they do shall result in your good.

Thomas Jefferson
Fourth Annual Message to Congress
March 4, 1805

President Jefferson's lifelong Bible studies were revealed in his message to the Congress and the American people as he began his second term as President.

I pray that Providence, in whose hands are the nations of the earth, may continue towards ours His fostering care, and bestow on yourselves the blessings of His protection and favor.

Thomas Jefferson
Letter to the Two Branches of
   the Legislature of Massachusetts
February 14, 1807

At this time, President Jefferson was seeking to protect the American merchant fleet (much of which sailed out of New England ports) from Britain's practice of "impressment" — stopping United States vessels and seizing sailors suspected of being deserters from the British navy. Writing to the predominantly Congregationalist members of the Massachusetts Legislature, he personalized his references to God.

I sincerely pray with you, my friends, that all the members of the human family may, in the time prescribed by the Father of us all, find themselves securely established in the enjoyment of life, liberty, and happiness.

> Thomas Jefferson
> Reply to Messrs. Thomas, Ellicot,
>   and others
> November 13, 1807

Like other leaders in the early years of the United States, President Jefferson regarded human history as occurring within a larger framework. In this letter, he expressed his desire to end slavery "at the first practicable moment."

Among the most inestimable of our blessings is that of liberty to worship our Creator in the way we think most agreeable to his will; a liberty deemed in other countries incompatible with good government, and yet proved by our experience to be its best support.

Thomas Jefferson
Letter to Captain John Thomas
November 18, 1807

Worship and adoration of God were encouraged by President Jefferson. However, he resisted imposition of specific religious beliefs on others.

We have all been encouraged to feel [that we are] in the guardianship and guidance of that Almighty Being whose power regulates the destiny of nations, whose blessings have been so conspicuously dispensed to this rising Republic, and to whom we are bound to address our devout gratitude for the past, as well as our fervent supplications and best hopes for the future.

James Madison
First Inaugural Address
March 4, 1809

The fourth President of the United States, James Madison — the prime mover in the separation of church and state by means of the First Amendment to the Constitution twenty years earlier — continued to regard worship of God as a duty. He had advanced that view in 1776 when he incorporated George Mason's words into the Virginia Declaration of Rights, and he had emphasized the same point in his "Memorial and Remonstrance" of 1785.

We are indebted to that Divine Providence whose goodness has been so remarkably extended to this rising nation. It becomes us to cherish a devout gratitude and to implore from the same omnipotent source a blessing on the consultations and measures about to be undertaken for the welfare of our beloved country.

James Madison
First Annual Message to Congress
November 29, 1809

Like the three Presidents who preceded him, James Madison called the attention of political leaders and ordinary citizens to the spiritual aspect of government and society.

Religion and virtue are the only foundations, not only of republicanism and of all free government, but of social felicity under all governments and in all the combinations of human society.

John Adams
Letter to Benjamin Rush
August 28, 1811

Retired, but not without opinions, John Adams discussed the importance of religion with his old friend, Benjamin Rush.

I recommend ... rendering the Sovereign of the Universe and the Benefactor of Mankind the public homage due to His holy attributes; of acknowledging the transgressions which might justly provoke the manifestations of His divine displeasure; of seeking His merciful forgiveness and His assistance in the great duties of repentance and amendment, and especially of offering fervent supplications that ... He would take the American people under His peculiar care and protection ... that He would inspire all nations with a love of justice and of concord and with a reverence for the unerring precept of our holy religion to do to others as they would require that others should do to them.

> James Madison
> Proclamation of a Day
>   of Humiliation and Prayer
> July 9, 1812

As the United States embarked upon a new war with Britain, President Madison's call for prayer was similar to the proclamations of the Continental Congress during the Revolutionary War more than thirty years earlier. These ceremonial statements were formal expressions of the private beliefs of the nation's leaders.

Of all the systems of morality, ancient or modern, which have come under my observation, none appear to me so pure as that of Jesus. He who follows this steadily need not, I think, be uneasy.

Thomas Jefferson
Letter to William Canby
September 18, 1813

Thomas Jefferson, retired from public office but now working to establish an institution of higher learning that would become the University of Virginia, had pursued a lifelong study of the Bible. This was a report of his findings.

[God] has formed us moral agents ... that we may promote the happiness of those with whom He has placed us in society, by acting honestly towards all, benevolently to those who fall within our way, respecting sacredly their rights, bodily and mental, and cherishing especially their freedom of conscience, as we value our own. I must ever believe that religion substantially good which produces an honest life, and we have been authorized by One whom you and I equally respect, to judge the tree by its fruit. Our particular principles of religion are a subject of accountability to our God alone.

> Thomas Jefferson
> Letter to Miles King
> September 26, 1814

Although often characterized as a deist who believed in a mechanistic universe set in motion by a "clockmaker God," Thomas Jefferson was concerned with issues of morality, religion and judgment throughout his life.

I recommend ... [that] all may have an opportunity of voluntarily offering, at the same time in their respective religious assemblies, their humble adoration to the Great Sovereign of the Universe, of confessing their sins and transgressions, and of strengthening their vows of repentance and amendment. A devout thankfulness ought to be mingled with their supplications to the Beneficent Parent of the Human Race that He would be graciously pleased to pardon all their offenses against Him.

James Madison
Proclamation of a Day of
    Humiliation, Fasting and Prayer
November 16, 1814

Near the conclusion of the war with Britain (the "War of 1812"), President Madison again called for national prayer.

No people ought to feel greater obligations to celebrate the goodness of the Great Disposer of Events and of the Destiny of Nations than the people of the United States. His kind providence originally conducted them to one of the best portions of the dwelling place allotted for the great family of the human race. He protected and cherished them under all the difficulties and trials to which they were exposed in their early days. Under His fostering care their habits, their sentiments, and their pursuits prepared them for a transition in due time to a state of independence and self-government. In the arduous struggle by which it was attained they were distinguished by multiplied tokens of His benign interposition.... And to the same Divine Author of Every Good and Perfect Gift we are indebted for all those privileges and advantages, religious as well as civil, which are so richly enjoyed in this favored land.

James Madison
Proclamation of a Day
    of Thanksgiving
March 4, 1815

Soon after the War of 1812 was officially terminated, President James Madison — whose ideas of government have been interpreted as excluding religion from public activities — called for the American people to acknowledge their obligations to God.

I have searched after truth by every means and by every opportunity in my power, and with a sincerity and impartiality, for which I can appeal to God, my adored Maker. My religion is founded on the love of God and my neighbor; on the hope of pardon for my offences; upon contrition; upon the duty as well as necessity of supporting with patience the inevitable evils of life; in the duty of doing no wrong, but all the good I can, to the creation of which I am but an infinitesimal part.

John Adams
Letter to F. A. Vanderkemp
July 13, 1815

In his retirement during the last years of James Madison's second administration, John Adams corresponded with friends and relatives on a wide variety of topics. Throughout his life, Adams often directed his thoughts to religion.

Real happiness ... depends on the love of God, a good conscience, and the exact and faithful discharge of the duties we owe to God and man.

Charles Carroll
Letter to Mary Patterson
October 23, 1816

One of Maryland's leading Patriots, Charles Carroll was the only Catholic signer of the Declaration of Independence. He had been selected as a delegate to the Continental Congress after helping to convince the Maryland Legislature to support separation of the Colonies from Britain. Motivated by his lifelong concern for religious freedom, he had participated in drafting and promoting the Bill of Rights as a Senator in the first Congress of the United States.

Without religion this world would be something not fit to be mentioned in polite company: I mean Hell.

John Adams
Letter to Thomas Jefferson
April 19, 1817

In their later years, John Adams and Thomas Jefferson renewed their earlier friendship, which had seemingly ended forever in the often bitter struggle between the Federalists, led by Adams (and Alexander Hamilton), and the Democratic Republicans, headed by Jefferson (with support from James Madison) during their terms as President. Brought back together by their mutual friend, Benjamin Rush, the two great Patriots continued their new correspondence until death — which occurred for both men on July 4, 1826, exactly fifty years after the Declaration of Independence.

I hold the precepts of Jesus, as delivered by himself, to be the most pure, benevolent, and sublime which have ever been preached to man.

Thomas Jefferson
Letter to Reverend Jared Sparks
November 4, 1820

Retired from public office, Thomas Jefferson devoted the remainder of his life to reading, correspondence and service as Rector of the University of Virginia, which had been established the previous year, largely as a result of his leadership.

Time indeed changes manners and notions, and so far we must expect institutions to bend to them. But time produces also corruption of principles, and against this it is the duty of good citizens to be ever on the watch.

> Thomas Jefferson
> Letter to Judge Spencer Roane
> March 9, 1821

How would Thomas Jefferson evaluate the changes in manners and notions since his time? Would he detect a corruption of principles?

Instruction in religious opinion and duties was not meant to be precluded by the public authorities as indifferent to the interests of society. On the contrary, the relations which exist between man and his Maker, and the duties resulting from those relations, are the most interesting and important to every human being, and the most incumbent on his study and investigation.

Thomas Jefferson
Report of the Board of Visitors
of the University of Virginia
October 7, 1822

Although Thomas Jefferson and James Madison (Jefferson's successor as President of the United States and as Rector of the University of Virginia) are often portrayed as hostile to religious instruction, they both considered that study to be highly valuable. In fact, Jefferson proposed sharing publicly-funded facilities with religious organizations.

(The original statement — *"It was not, however, to be understood that* instruction in religious opinions and duties was meant to be precluded by the public authorities as indifferent to the interests of society." — has been edited for clarity by taking the *"not"* from the phrase highlighted with italics and inserting it before "meant" in the sentence at the top of the page. The full text is printed on page 229.)

Adore God. Reverence and cherish your parents. Love your neighbor as yourself, and your country more than yourself. Be just. Be true. Murmur not at the ways of Providence. So shall the life, into which you have entered, be the portal to one of eternal and ineffable bliss. And if to the dead it is permitted to care for the things of this world, every action of your life will be under my regard. Farewell.

Thomas Jefferson
Letter to Thomas Jefferson Smith
February 21, 1825

The year before his death at age 83, Thomas Jefferson offered this advice to his infant grandson.

Man was destined for two worlds — the one of transient, and the other of perpetual, duration. His welfare in both depends on his acceptance and use of the means for obtaining it, which his merciful Creator has for that purpose appointed and ordained.... These inestimable and unmerited blessings ... by the direction and inspiration of their Divine Author ... were specified and recorded in the Bible.

As these gracious dispensations provide for our consolation ... in this life and for our perfect and endless felicity in the next, no communications can be of higher or more general interest.

>John Jay
>Address to the American
> Bible Society
>May 12, 1825

John Jay — formerly a member of the Continental Congress, diplomat, Chief Justice of the Supreme Court of the United States, and Governor of New York — used his retirement years to promote the American Bible Society, serving as its President from 1821 until his death eight years later.

The belief in a God, all powerful, wise, and good, is so essential to the moral order of the world, and to the happiness of man, that arguments which enforce it cannot be drawn from too many sources.

James Madison
Letter to Reverend F. Beasley
November 20, 1825

These words were written by the individual credited with erecting what Thomas Jefferson termed "a wall of separation between church and state."

The context of Jefferson's famous phrase — included in a letter to the Baptist Association of Danbury, Connecticut — will be found on page 200.

I express my earnest hope that the peace, happiness, and prosperity enjoyed by our beloved country may induce those who direct our national councils to recommend a general and public return of praise and thanksgiving to Him from whose goodness these blessings descend.

The most effectual means of securing the continuance of our civil and religious liberties is always to remember with reverence and gratitude the source from which they flow.

> John Jay
> Letter to the Committee
>   of the Corporation
>   of the City of New York
> June 29, 1826

These were John Jay's words in response to an invitation to speak during New York's celebration of the fiftieth anniversary of the Declaration of Independence. That day would mark the close of an era with the deaths of John Adams and Thomas Jefferson.

Additional Words

From Our Nation's Founders

God Has Blessed America

For our nation's founders, faith in God went well beyond a gentle hope that America would receive heavenly blessings. Their writings show that our early leaders held a stronger belief: God manifested His will in history, and a nation that honestly sought to conform itself to the dictates of the Almighty would enjoy His blessings.

Certainly they were not alone in that belief; but as they witnessed the optimistic energy of the American people and the success of the new form of government, they concluded that this nation had indeed been greatly blessed — and they gave their thanks to God. During times of distress and peril, they prayed for forgiveness and deliverance. They turned to God in good times and bad.

Their belief in God's blessing on America can be found in their own words:

> The second day of July 1776 [when independence was approved by the Continental Congress, two days before the final wording of the declaration could be resolved] will be the most memorable date in the history of America. I am apt to believe that it will be celebrated by succeeding generations as the great anniversary festival. It ought to be commemorated, as the Day of Deliverance by solemn acts of devotion to God Almighty. It ought to be solemnized with pomp and parade, with shows, games, sports, guns, bells, bonfires and illuminations from one end of this continent to the other from this time forward forever more....

I am well aware of the toil and blood and treasure that it will cost us to maintain this Declaration, and support and defend these States. Yet through all the gloom I can see the rays of ravishing light and glory. I can see that the end is more than worth all the means — and that posterity will triumph in that day's transaction.

John Adams
Letter to Abigail Adams
July 3, 1776

* * *

The Americans are the first people whom Heaven has favored with an opportunity of deliberating upon and choosing the forms of government under which they should live. All other constitutions have derived their existence from violence or accidental circumstances, and are therefore probably more distant from their perfection, which, though beyond our reach, may nevertheless be approached under the guidance of reason and experience.

John Jay
Charge to the Grand Jury
  of Ulster County, New York
September 9, 1777

God has been pleased to bless our endeavors, in a just cause, with remarkable success. To us upon the spot, who have seen, step by step, the progress of this great contest ... we seem to have been treading upon enchanted ground.

George Mason
Letter to Mr. Brent
October 2, 1778

* * *

We ... acknowledge, with grateful hearts, the goodness of the great Legislator of the universe, in affording us, in the course of His providence, an opportunity, deliberately and peaceably, without fraud, violence, or surprise, of entering into an original, explicit, and solemn compact with each other ... devoutly imploring His direction.

Massachusetts Constitution
(Drafted by John Adams)
March 2, 1780

The providential train of circumstances ... affords the most convincing proof that the liberties of America are the object of divine Protection.

George Washington
Orders to the Continental Army
September 26, 1780

* * *

The citizens of America, placed in the most enviable condition, ... are now acknowledged to be possessed of absolute freedom and independence. They are, from this period, to be considered as the actors on a most conspicuous theater, which seems to be peculiarly designated by Providence for the display of human greatness and felicity. Here, they are not only surrounded with every thing which can contribute to the completion of private and domestic enjoyment, but Heaven has crowned all its other blessings, by giving a fairer opportunity for political happiness, than any other nation has ever been favored with.

George Washington
Circular Letter to the States
June 8, 1783

I have ever turned my eye, with a fixed confidence on that superintending Providence which governs all events, and the lively gratitude I now feel is beyond my expression....

So great a revolution as this country now experiences, doubtless ranks high in the scale of human events, and in the eye of Omnipotence is introductive to some noble scenes of future grandeur to this happy fated continent....

I pray that Heaven, from the stores of its munificence, may shower its choicest blessings on you and to entreat that our liberties, now so happily established, may be continued in perfect security, to the latest posterity.

> George Washington
> Letter to the Massachusetts Senate
>   and House of Representatives
> August 10, 1783

* * *

I attribute all the glory to that Supreme Being ... who was able by the humblest instruments as well as by the most powerful means to establish and secure the liberty and happiness of these United States.

> George Washington
> Letter to the inhabitants of Princeton
>   and neighborhood
> August 25, 1783

It would be improper to omit, in this first official act, my fervent supplications to that Almighty Being who rules over the universe, who presides in the councils of nations, and whose providential aids can supply every human defect, that His benediction may consecrate to the liberties and happiness of the people of the United States, a government instituted by themselves for these essential purposes.... In tendering this homage to the Great Author of every public and private good, I assure myself that it expresses your sentiments not less than my own.... No people can be bound to acknowledge and adore the invisible hand which conducts the affairs of men more than the people of the United States. Every step by which they have advanced to the character of an independent nation seems to have been distinguished by some token of providential agency.

George Washington
First Inaugural Address
April 30, 1789

When we contemplate the coincidence of circumstances and wonderful combination of causes which gradually prepared the people of this country for independence ... we are unavoidably led to acknowledge and adore the Great Arbiter of the Universe, by whom empires rise and fall. A review of the many signal instances of Divine interposition in favor of this country claims our most pious gratitude.

> United States Senate
> Address to George Washington
> May 7, 1789

* * *

I hope and trust that Providence will continue to bless us with as much prosperity as will be good for us.

> John Jay
> Letter to the Rev. Dr. Thatcher
> May 26, 1796

* * *

I pray that [our country] may experience a continuance of the Divine blessings, by which it has been so signally favored.

> James Madison
> Message to Congress
> May 23, 1809

A proper history of the United States would have much to recommend it: in some respects it would be singular, or unlike all others; it would develop the great plan of Providence.... In my opinion, the historian, in the course of the work, is never to lose sight of that great plan.

Remarkable interpositions of Divine Providence are fine subjects.

John Jay
Letter to the Rev. Dr. Morse
August 16, 1809

* * *

I was borne along by an irresistible sense of duty. God prospered our labors; and ... I hope that the ultimate good of the world, of the human race, and of our beloved country, is intended and will be accomplished by it.

John Adams
Letter to Benjamin Rush
August 28, 1811

Liberty, Virtue and Duty

Our nation's founders recognized that freedom depends on public virtue. And, as their writings have shown, they perceived an important linkage between virtue and religious principles.

Nevertheless, a distinction between virtue and religion was assumed. In the first edition (1828) of his *American Dictionary of the English Language*, Noah Webster — a friend of many of the leaders of the new democratic republic — supplied the definitions (and examples of usage) for his time:

VIRTUE: Moral goodness.

The practice of moral duties merely from motives of convenience or from compulsion, or from regard for reputation, is *virtue* as distinct from *religion*. The practice of moral duties from sincere love of God and His laws is virtue *and* religion.

DUTY: That which a person owes to another; that which a person is bound, by any natural, moral or legal obligation, to pay, do or perform.

Reverence, obedience and prayer to God are indispensible *duties*.

Webster was the first lexicographer to base his definitions on actual American usage. He was well aware that the Presidents of his day — George Washington, John Adams, Thomas Jefferson and James Madison — together with the other advocates and builders of this nation, regarded civic virtue as essential. In fact, he corresponded with many of the country's leaders and studied their ideas. His writings reveal that he also shared their fundamental belief, based on a common reading of history, that virtue without a religious foundation was subject to shifting definitions and lapses in practice; therefore, both civic virtue and religion must be encouraged.

The founders' reliance on God was transformed into a positive duty to preserve their heavenly gift, freedom. In their own words:

Virtue is the surest means of securing the public liberty.... Every thing that we do, or ought to esteem valuable, depends upon it. For freedom or slavery ... will prevail in a country according as the disposition and manners of the inhabitants render them fit for the one or the other.

Samuel Adams
Letter to Elbridge Gerry
October 29, 1775

＊ ＊ ＊

All agree our claims are righteous and must be supported. Yet all, or at least too great a part among us, withhold the means, as if Providence, who has already done much for us, would continue His gracious interposition and work miracles for our deliverance, without troubling ourselves about the matter.

George Washington
Letter to Brigadier General
Samuel Holden Parsons
April 23, 1777

We are contending for the liberty and happiness of our own country and posterity. It is a glorious contest. We shall succeed if we are virtuous. I am infinitely more apprehensive of the contagion of vice than the power of all other enemies.

> Samuel Adams
> Letter to John Langdon
> August 7, 1777

* * *

A general dissolution of principles and manners will more surely overthrow the liberties of America than the whole force of the common enemy. While the people are virtuous they cannot be subdued; but when once they lose their virtue they will be ready to surrender their liberties to the first external or *internal* invader. How necessary is it for those who are determined to transmit the blessings of liberty as a fair inheritance to posterity, to associate on public principles in support of public virtue.... If virtue and knowledge are diffused among the people, they will never be enslaved. This will be their great security. Virtue and knowledge will forever be an even balance for powers and riches. I hope our countrymen will never depart from the principles and maxims which have been handed down to us from our wise forefathers. This greatly depends upon the example of men of character and influence of the present day.

> Samuel Adams
> Letter to James Warren
> February 12, 1779

At best I have only been an instrument in the hands of Providence.... [Our] country may afford an asylum, if we are wise enough to pursue the paths which lead to virtue and happiness, to the oppressed and needy of the earth. Our region is extensive, our plains are productive, and if they are cultivated with liberality and good sense, we may be happy ourselves, and diffuse happiness to all who wish to participate.

> George Washington
> Letter to Lucretia Wilhemina
> Van Winter
> March 30, 1785

* * *

Next to the duty which young men owe to their Creator, I wish to see a regard to their country inculcated upon them.

> Benjamin Rush
> *A Plan for Establishing Public Schools*
> *in Pennsylvania*
> 1786

What is the efficient cause of moral obligation? The will of God. This is the supreme law. His just and full right of imposing laws, and our duty in obeying them, are the sources of our moral obligations.

James Wilson
Lectures on Law: Law and Obligation
1790

* * *

Peace we estimate as one of the most precious gifts of Heaven, and with heartfelt emotions of gratitude we adore the Ruler of nations for our long, uninterrupted enjoyment of it; but basely to pursue this blessing at the expense of our liberty is undutiful, not only to ourselves, but also to that benignant Deity who decreed that man should be free. The moment that an individual or a nation passively receives the insults of oppression, they sink from that elevation of character for which they were originally destined.

The Inhabitants of Washington
County, New York
Address to John Jay
August 9, 1798

We should proceed in doing good because it is our duty and not from the hope or expectation of grateful returns. Except in certain particular cases, it is better to "cast our bread on the waters," that is, on many; here a little, and there a little, according to our abilities and opportunities, and leave the result to Providence.

John Jay
Letter to his Children
1810

Freedom of Religion:
From Religion or *For* Religion?

The founders of this nation were rebels as well as builders, and the targets of that rebellion included many religious institutions of their day. The American opponents of tyranny were keen observers of European history, which had recorded the frequent connection between authoritarian government and a single religion endorsed and enforced by the state. In fact, the "religious wars" in Europe — characterized by torture, mass deportations, starvation and humiliation of captured foes because of their different manner of worshipping God in the name of Jesus Christ — had occurred only some one hundred and thirty years before the Declaration of Independence. (By way of comparison, the American Civil War took place just 130 years ago.)

To assure their own right to worship God in the manner that each individual believed to be proper — and to guarantee that "first freedom" to all citizens of the new nation — our nation's founders made a clear distinction between matters of church and state. No denomination or sect would be given preference in the new government, and the state would not be permitted to interfere in the worship of God by any person or group.

They sought to protect the connection between God and His people, not banish Him from the American scene. In fact, James Madison, the author of the First Amendment, concurred with George Mason's first draft of the Virginia Declaration of Rights, which declared that worship is "the duty that we owe to our Creator."

Today, the First Amendment is often cited as a guarantee of "freedom *from* religion." When it was

197

ratified some two hundred years ago, this vital addition to the Constitution assured freedom *for* religion. No denomination or sect would be permitted to dominate other forms of worship and fellowship. No matter how small or unpopular the congregation, religious observances were protected from interference by the government. As far as the state was concerned, each individual could choose his or her manner of relating to God — including the right to avoid all established religious bodies.

Because of the importance of religious ideas in their own lives, the founders of the United States were not attempting to build a wall of separation between the people and God. Instead, they wished to assure that each individual could find his path to God without interference by the government or by a domineering religious establishment.

Their own words help to reveal their views:

Religion, or the duty which we owe to our divine and omnipotent Creator, and the manner of discharging it, can be governed only by reason and conviction.... It is the mutual duty of all to practice Christian forbearance, love, and charity towards each other.

George Mason
Virginia Declaration of Rights
(First Draft)
May, 1776

The rights of conscience we never submitted, we could not submit. We are answerable for them to our God.

> Thomas Jefferson
> *Notes on Virginia*, Query XVII
> 1781

* * *

The sacred obligations of religion flow from the due exercise of opinion, in the solemn discharge of which man is accountable to his God alone.

> James Madison
> Address of the General Assembly to
>   the People of the Commonwealth
>   of Virginia
> January 23, 1799

* * *

I promised you a letter on Christianity, which I have not forgotten.... I have a view of the subject which ought to displease neither the rational Christian nor Deists, and would reconcile many to a character they have too hastily rejected.... As every sect believes its own form the true one, every one perhaps hoped for his own [to become the established religion in the United States].... The returning good sense of our country threatens abortion to their hopes, and they believe that any portion of power confided to me will be exerted in opposition to their schemes. And they believe rightly: For I have sworn upon the altar of God eternal hostility against every form of tyranny over the mind of man. But this is all they have to fear from me — and enough, too, in their opinion.

Thomas Jefferson
Letter to Benjamin Rush
September 23, 1800

* * *

Believing with you that religion is a matter which lies solely between man and his God, that he owes account to none other for his faith or his worship, that the legislative powers of government reach actions only, and not opinions, I contemplate with sovereign reverence the act of the whole American people which declared that their legislature should "make no law respecting an establishment of religion, or prohibiting the free exercise thereof," thus building a wall of separation between church and State. Adhering to this expression of the supreme will of the nation in behalf of the rights of conscience, I shall see with sincere satisfaction the progress of those sentiments which tend to restore to man all his natural rights, convinced he has no natural right in opposition to his social duties.

I reciprocate your kind prayers for the protection and blessing of the common Father and Creator of man and tender you for yourselves and your religious associations assurances of my high respect and esteem.

Thomas Jefferson
Letter to the Danbury, Connecticut
Baptist Association
January 1, 1802

* * *

In our early struggles for liberty, religious freedom could not fail to become a primary object. All men felt the right, and a just animation to obtain it was exhibited by all. I was one only among the many who befriended its establishment, and am entitled but in common with others to a portion of that approbation which follows the fulfillment of a duty....

The principles which justified us were obvious to all understandings. They were imprinted in the breast of every human being; and Providence ever pleases to direct the issue of our content in favor of that side where justice was....

A recollection of our former vassalage in religion and civil government will unite the zeal of every heart, and the energy of every hand, to preserve that independence in both which, under the favor of heaven, a disinterested devotion to the pubic cause first achieved and a disinterested sacrifice of private interests will now maintain....

I return your kind prayers with supplications to the same almighty Being for your future welfare and that of our beloved country.

> Thomas Jefferson
> Letter to the Baltimore, Maryland
>   Baptist Association
> October 17, 1808

* * *

If the public homage of a people can ever be worthy of the favorable regard of the Holy and Omniscient Being to whom it is addressed, it must be when those who join in it are guided only by their free choice, by the impulse of their hearts and the dictates of their consciences; and such a spectacle must be interesting to all Christian nations as proving that religion, that gift of Heaven for the good of man, freed from all coercive edicts ... can spread its benign influence everywhere and can attract to the divine altar those freewill offerings of humble supplication, thanksgiving, and praise which alone can be acceptable to Him whom no hypocrisy can deceive and no forced sacrifices propitiate.

> James Madison
> A Proclamation of a Day
>   of Humiliation and Prayer
> July 23, 1813

Christianity
And Our Nation's Founders

Virtually all of the founders of this nation grew up in a Christian environment, supported Christian churches, and assumed a Christian value system. Therefore, they seldom saw the need to make statements concerning their Christian beliefs.

Speakers and writers have never prefaced their remarks by declaring, "As a life-long resident of the planet Earth ..." or "My extensive experience as a human being assures me ...." At the time that our nation's founders were devising and establishing the form of government we are privileged to enjoy, it was usually unnecessary to state the obvious: "As a Christian ...."

For the most part, our early leaders purposely withheld public comments about personal religious convictions. As architects and builders of a new democratic republic in America — an experimental form of government based on participation of the general populace — they were usually careful not to suggest a sectarian preference in order to avoid injecting religious differences into the difficult political process that was just being tested.

Nevertheless, several of the Founding Fathers volunteered a few words about their personal beliefs:

[The] greatest concern [of the first planters in these Colonies] seems to have been to establish a government of the church more consistent with the Scriptures, and a government of the state more agreeable to the dignity of human nature ... and to transmit such a government down to their posterity, with the means of securing and

203

preserving it forever. [They endeavored] to render the popular power in their new government as great and wise as ... human nature and the Christian religion require it should be.... And in this they discovered the depth of their wisdom and the warmth of their friendship to human nature. But the first place is due to religion.

> John Adams
> *Dissertation on the Canon*
> *and the Feudal Law*
> August, 1765

* * *

We are the descendents of ancestors remarkable for their zeal for true religion and liberty.... Here they resolved to set up the worship of God, according to their best judgement, upon the plan of the New Testament; to maintain it among themselves, and transmit it to their posterity.... They were prospered in their settlement by Him, whose is the earth and the fullness thereof, beyond all human expectation.

> Samuel Adams
> Letter to "Reverend G. W."
> November 11, 1765

To be possessed of the Christian principles, and to accommodate our whole deportment to such principles, is to be happy in this life; it is this that sweetens everything we enjoy.

Samuel Adams
Letter to Andrew Elton Wells
October 21, 1772

* * *

You will judge it quite necessary that we should assert [and] vindicate our rights as Christians as well as men....

May God grant that the love of liberty and a zeal to support it may enkindle in every town.

Samuel Adams
Letter to Elbridge Gerry
November 14, 1772

Desirous to have people of all ranks and degrees duly impressed with a solemn sense of God's superintending Providence, and of their duty devoutly to rely in all their lawful enterprises on His aid and direction, [the Congress] earnestly recommends that we confess and bewail our manifold sins and transgressions, and, by a sincere repentance and amendment of life, appease His righteous displeasure, and through the merits and meditation of Jesus Christ obtain his pardon and forgiveness — that He would be pleased to bless all his people with health and plenty, and grant that a spirit of incorruptible patriotism, and of pure undefiled religion, may universally prevail.

> Continental Congress
> Proclamation of a Day of
>   Humiliation, Fasting and Prayer
> (Prepared by William Livingston)
> March 16, 1776

✳ ✳ ✳

The blessing and protection of heaven are at all times necessary but especially so in times of public distress and danger. The General hopes and trusts that every officer and man will endeavor to live, and act, as becomes a Christian soldier defending the dearest rights and liberties of his country.

> George Washington
> Orders to the Continental Army
> July 9, 1776

I do believe in one God, the creator and governor of the universe, the rewarder of the good and the punisher of the wicked. And I do acknowledge the Scriptures of the Old and New Testament to be given by Divine inspiration.

Constitution of Pennsylvania:
Oath of Allegiance
Benjamin Franklin, President
of the Convention
July 15, 1776

* * *

The [delegates to the] convention by whom the constitution was formed were of the opinion that the gospel of Christ, like the ark of God, would not fall, though unsupported by the arm of flesh; and happy would it be for mankind if that opinion prevailed more generally....

Let virtue, honor, the love of liberty and of science be and remain the soul of this constitution, and it will become the source of great and extensive happiness to this and future generations. Vice, ignorance, and want of vigilance will be the only enemies able to destroy it.... Every member of the State ought diligently to read and to study the constitution of his country, and teach the rising generation to be free. By knowing their rights, they will sooner perceive when they are violated, and be the better prepared to defend and assert them.

John Jay
Charge to the Grand Jury
of Ulster County, New York
September 9, 1777

It is therefore recommended ... that at one time, and with one voice, the good people may express the grateful feelings of their hearts, and consecrate themselves to the service of their divine Benefactor. And, that together with their sincere acknowledgements and offerings, they may join the penitent confession of their manifold sins, whereby they had forfeited every favor; and their humble and earnest supplication that it may please God through the merits of Jesus Christ mercifully to forgive and blot them out of remembrance — that it may please Him graciously to afford His blessing on the governments of these States and to prosper the council of the whole [Congress] — to inspire our commanders both by land and sea, and all under them with that wisdom and fortitude which may render them fit instruments, under the Providence of Almighty God, to secure for these United States, the greatest of all human blessings, independence and peace — that it may please Him ... to take schools and seminaries of education, so necessary for cultivating the principles of true liberty, virtue, and piety, under His nurturing hand; and to prosper the means of religion for the promotion and enlargement of that kingdom which consisted "in righteousness peace and joy in the Holy Ghost."

Samuel Adams
Draft Resolution for
    the Continental Congress
November 1, 1777

It is recommended that together with devout thanksgivings may be joined a penitent confession of our sins, and humble supplication for pardon through the merits of our Savior — so that under the smiles of Heaven, our public councils may be directed ... — our schools and seminaries of learning flourish — ... and the hearts of all impressed with genuine piety, with benevolence, and zeal for the public good.

> Samuel Adams
> Draft Resolution for the
>   Continental Congress
> November 3, 1778

* * *

The encouragement of arts and sciences, and all good literature, tends to the honor of God, the advantage of the Christian religion, and the great benefit of this and the other United States of America.

> Massachusetts Constitution
> (Drafted by John Adams)
> March 2, 1780

A Christian cannot fail of being a republican, for every precept of the Gospel inculcates those degrees of humility, self-denial, and brotherly kindness, which are directly opposed to the pride of monarchy and the pageantry of a court. A Christian cannot fail of being useful to the republic, for his religion teaches him, that no man "liveth to himself."

Benjamin Rush
A Plan for Establishing Public Schools in Pennsylvania
1786

* * *

The Christian religion is ... the religion of wisdom, virtue, equity, and humanity.... It is resignation to God. It is goodness itself to man.

John Adams
Diary (in *Autobiography*)
July 26, 1796

One great advantage of the Christian religion is that it brings the great principle of the law of nature and nations: love your neighbor as yourself, and do to others as you would that others should do to you — to the knowledge, belief, and veneration of the whole people. Children, servants, women, and men, are all professors in the science of public and private morality. No other institution for education, no kind of political discipline, could diffuse this kind of necessary information, so universally among all ranks and descriptions of citizens. The duties and rights of the man and the citizen are thus taught from early infancy to every creature. The sanctions of a future life are thus added to the observance of civil and political, as well as domestic and private duties. Prudence, justice, temperance, and fortitude are thus taught to be the means and conditions of future as well as present happiness.

John Adams
Diary (in *Autobiography*)
August 14, 1796

Together with our thanksgiving, earnest supplication to God is hereby recommended for the forgiveness of our sins which have rendered us unworthy of the least of His mercies; and that by the sanctifying influence of His spirit, our hearts and manners may be corrected, and we become a reformed and happy people — that He would direct and prosper the administration of the government of the United States ... — that tyranny and usurpation may everywhere come to an end — that the nations who are contending for true liberty may still be succeeded by his Almighty aid — that every nation and society of men may be inspired with the knowledge and feeling of their natural and just rights, and enabled to form such systems of civil government as shall be fully adopted to promote and establish their social security and happiness — and, finally, that in the course of God's Holy Providence, the great family of mankind may bow to the scepter of the Prince of Peace so that mutual friendship and harmony may universally prevail.

Samuel Adams
Proclamation of the Governor
of Massachusetts
October 17, 1796

[I have] an unshaken confidence in the honor, spirit, and resource of the American people, on which I have so often hazarded my all, and never been deceived; elevated ideas of the high destinies of this country, and of my own duties towards it, founded on a knowledge of the moral principles and intellectual improvements of the people ...; a veneration for the religion of a people who profess and call themselves Christians; and a fixed resolution to consider a decent respect for Christianity among the best recommendations for the public service.

> John Adams
> Inaugural Speech to Both
>   Houses of Congress
> March 4, 1797

It having been the invariable practice derived from the days of our renowned ancestors ... [I] earnestly recommend to the ministers of the Gospel with their respective congregations to assemble together and with one united voice confess our past sins and transgressions, with holy resolutions, by the Grace of God, to turn our feet into the path of His Law — humbly beseeching him to endue us with all the Christian spirit of piety, benevolence and the love of our country....

And as it is our duty to extend our wishes to the happiness of the great family of man, we cannot better express ourselves than by humbly supplicating the Supreme Ruler of the World — that the rod of tyrants may be broken into pieces, and the oppressed made free — that wars may cease in all the earth — and that the confusions that are and have been among the nations may be overruled for the promoting and speedily bringing on that holy and happy period, when the kingdom of our Lord and Saviour Jesus Christ may be everywhere established, and all the people willingly bow to the Scepter of Him who is the Prince of Peace.

Samuel Adams
Proclamation of the
   Governor of Massachusetts
March 20, 1797

Jesus embraced with charity and philanthropy our neighbors, our countrymen, and the whole family of mankind.

Thomas Jefferson
Letter to Edward Dowse, Esq.
April 19, 1803

* * *

I am a Christian ... sincerely attached to His doctrines, in preference to all others.

Thomas Jefferson
Letter to Benjamin Rush
April 21, 1803

* * *

The Christian religion, as I understand it, is the brightness of the glory and the express portrait of the character of the eternal, self-existent, independent, benevolent, all powerful and all merciful Creator, Preserver, and Father of the universe, the first good, first perfect, and first fair. It will last as long as the world.

John Adams
Letter to Benjamin Rush
January 21, 1810

I am reminded ... of your synopsis of the four Evangelists.... I, too, have made a wee-little book from the same materials, which I call the Philosophy of Jesus.... A more beautiful or precious morsel of ethics I have never seen; it is a document in proof that I am a real Christian, that is to say, a disciple of the doctrines of Jesus.

Thomas Jefferson
Letter to Charles Thomson
January 9, 1816

* * *

It certainly is very desirable that a pacific disposition should prevail among all nations. The most effectual way of producing it is by extending the prevalence and influence of the gospel. Real Christians will abstain from violating the rights of others, and therefore will not provoke war.

John Jay
Letter to John Murray, Jr.
October 12, 1816

Jesus is benevolence personified, an example for all men.... The Christian religion, in its primitive purity and simplicity, I have entertained for more than sixty years. It is the religion of reason, equity, and love; it is the religion of the head and of the heart.

John Adams
Letter to F. A. Vanderkemp
December 27, 1816

* * *

If the sublime doctrines ... taught us by Jesus of Nazareth, in which all agree, constitute true religion, then, without it, this would be, as you say, "something not fit to be named, even indeed, a hell."

Thomas Jefferson
Letter to John Adams
May 5, 1817

Indeed, Jesus himself, the founder of our religion, was unquestionably a materialist as to man. In all his doctrines of the resurrection, he teaches expressly that the body is to rise in substance. In the apostles' creed, we all declare that we believe in the "resurrection of the body."

Thomas Jefferson
Letter to Mr. Woodward
March 24, 1824

Benjamin Franklin on Religion: "Now I Speak of Thanking God"

Benjamin Franklin has often been portrayed as indifferent to religion — even an opponent of worship. That description is accurate only in one sense: he was impatient with the doctrinal disputes and the contests for supremacy that occupied so much church life of his time. Despite his preference for study and devotion at home, he was a consistent financial supporter of the churches in Philadelphia, and he strongly urged his daughter to attend services in order to develop the proper appreciation of religious worship.

His particularly memorable statements regarding prayer and the positive attributes of Christianity are found elsewhere in this book (such as pages 1, 4, 9, 100 and 110). A more complete understanding of his views concerning God and religious practices is revealed by the following prayers and statements:

O wise God, my good Father!

Thou behold the sincerity of my heart and of my devotion; grant me a continuance of thy favor!

...

Thou abhor in thy creatures treachery and deceit, malice, revenge, and every other hurtful vice; but Thou art a lover of justice and sincerity, of friendship and benevolence, and every virtue. Thou art my Friend, my Father, and my Benefactor.— Praised be thy name, O God, forever! Amen!

"Adoration"
(Personal Papers)
November 20, 1728

That I may be sincere in friendship, faithful in trust, and impartial in judgment, watchful against pride, and against anger (that momentary madness), — Help me, O Father! ...

That I may be just in all my dealings, temperate in my pleasures, full of candor and ingenuity, humanity and benevolence, — Help me, O Father! ...

That I may possess integrity and evenness of mind, resolution in difficulties, and fortitude under affliction; that I may be punctual in performing my promises, peaceable and prudent in my behavior, — Help me, O Father! ...

That I may have tenderness for the weak, and reverent respect for the ancient; that I may be kind to my neighbors, good-natured to my companions, and hospitable to strangers, — Help me, O Father!

"Petition" (Personal Papers)
November 20, 1728

* * *

The Scriptures assure me that at the last day we shall not be examined what we thought, but what we did; and our recommendation will not be that we said, Lord! Lord! but that we did good to our fellow creatures.

Letter to Josiah Franklin
April 13, 1738

The good education of youth has been esteemed by wise men in all ages, as the surest foundation of the happiness both of private families and of commonwealths. Almost all governments have therefore made it a principal object of their attention, to establish and endow with proper revenues, such seminaries of learning, as might supply the succeeding age with men qualified to serve the public with honor to themselves, and to their country....

History will also afford frequent opportunities of showing the necessity of a public religion, from its usefulness to the public; the advantage of a religious character among private persons; ... and the excellency of the Christian religion above all others ancient or modern....

The idea of what is true merit should also be often presented to youth, explained and impressed on their minds as consisting in an inclination joined with an ability to serve mankind, one's country, friends and family; which ability is (with the blessing of God) to be acquired or greatly increased by true learning; and should indeed be the great aim and end of all learning.

> *Proposals Relating to the Education*
> *of Youth in Pennsylvania*
> 1749

When I am employed in serving others, I do not look upon myself as conferring favors, but as paying debts. In my travels, and since my settlement, I have received much kindness from men, to whom I shall never have any opportunity of making the least direct return — and numberless mercies from God, who is infinitely above being benefited by our services. Those kindnesses from men, I can therefore only return on their fellow men; and I can only show my gratitude for these mercies from God by a readiness to help his other children and my brethren. For I do not think that thanks and compliments, tho' repeated weekly, can discharge our real obligations to each other, and much less those to our Creator. You will see in this my notion of good works, that I am far from expecting to merit Heaven by them....

The worship of God is a duty; the hearing and reading of sermons may be useful; but, if men rest in hearing and praying, as too many do, it is as if a tree should value itself on being watered and putting forth leaves, though it never produced any fruit.

Letter to Joseph Huey
June 6, 1753

Now I speak of thanking God. I desire with all humility to acknowledge that I owe the happiness of my past life to His kind providence, which led me to the means I used and gave them success. My belief of this induces me to hope, though I must not presume, that the same goodness will still be exercised toward me, in continuing that happiness, or enabling me to bear a fatal reverse.

Autobiography
1771

* * *

Anyone ... will see abundant reason to bless Divine Providence for the evident and great difference in our favor and be convinced that no nation that is known to us enjoys a greater share of human felicity....

Be quiet and thankful.

The Internal State of America
1786

A Note on Providence

Some historians assert that the word "Providence" is interchangeable with "good luck" or "good fortune." Therefore, they claim that the frequent use of this word by George Washington and other early leaders of our nation is evidence that they regarded God as a remote, impersonal Deity.

The quotations in this book reveal quite a different meaning. For example, George Washington referred to Providence and then, in the same statement, to "His gracious interposition." In other instances, our first President used the same word (without capitalization) to denote God's assistance or intervention. Both meanings were considered entirely proper in Washington's day, and both were based on an understanding that God's will is manifested in the real world.

Noah Webster's renowned *American Dictionary of the English Language* (1828) provided the following explanation:

PROVIDENCE:

In theology, the care and superintendence which God exercises over His creatures. He that acknowledges a creation and denies a *providence* involves himself in a palpable contradiction; for the same power that causes a thing to exist is necessary to continue its existence. Some persons admit a *general providence*, but deny a *particular providence*, not considering that a *general providence* consists of *particulars*. A belief in divine *providence* is a source of great consolation to good men. *Divine Providence* is often understood [as] God Himself.

Benjamin Rush:
The Commentator of His Day

One of the most prominent personalities in the formative years of this nation, Benjamin Rush was a prolific commentator. He was also one of the leading physicians in America, a signer of the Declaration of Independence, a promoter of the Constitution of the United States, a friend of Presidents from both political parties, Treasurer of the United States Mint for sixteen years, and a driving force in the American Philosophical Society. His views were so widely respected that he was given the honor of presenting the Fourth of July oration in Philadelphia when the Constitutional Convention was assembled there.

Doctor Rush frequently offered his advice to the nation:

> Those philosophers who reject Christianity, and those Christians, whether parents or school-masters, who neglect the religious instruction of their children and pupils, reject and neglect the most effectual means of promoting knowledge in our country....
>
> If the measures that have been recommended [in this essay] for inspiring our pupils with a sense of religious and moral obligation are adopted, the government of them will be easy and agreeable. Strictness of discipline will always render severity unnecessary. There will be the most instruction in that school where there is the most order.

> *Thoughts Upon Female Education*
> July 28, 1787

I have sometimes been led ... to suspect that the melioration of our world is to be brought about not so much by the improvements of human reason as by a faithful imitation of the example of our Saviour and a general obedience to the plain and humble precepts of the Gospel. But why do I prefer these to the improvements of reason? Reason accords with them all, and its brightest improvement consists in obeying the doctrines and obeying the precepts of the Christian religion.

Letter to John Coakley Lettsom
September 28, 1787

* * *

From the success or failure of your exertions in the cause of virtue, we anticipate the freedom or slavery of our country. Even the government of the United States, from which so many advantages are expected, will neither restore order nor establish justice among us unless it be accompanied and supported by morality among all classes of people.

Address to the Ministers of the
Gospel of all Denominations
June 21, 1788

But alas! my friend, I fear all our attempts to produce political happiness by the solitary influence of human reason will be as fruitless as the search for the philosopher's stone. It seems to be reserved to Christianity alone to produce universal, moral, political, and physical happiness. Reason produces, it is true, great and popular truths, but it affords motives too feeble to induce mankind to act agreeably to them. Christianity unfolds the same truths and accompanies them with motives, agreeable, powerful, and irresistible.

Letter to Noah Webster
July 20, 1798

* * *

The Gospel of Jesus Christ prescribes the wisest rules for just conduct in every situation of life. Happy they who are enabled to obey them in all situations!

Travels Through Life
1800

By renouncing the Bible, philosophers swing from their moorings upon all moral subjects.... It is the only correct map of the human heart that ever has been published. It contains a faithful representation of all its follies, vices, and crimes. All systems of religion, morals, and government not founded upon it must perish, and how consoling the thought — it will not only survive the wreck of these systems but the world itself.

> Letter to John Adams
> January 23, 1807

* * *

Man is as necessarily a praying [animal] as he is a sociable, domestic, or religious animal. As "no man liveth and sinneth not," so no man liveth and prayeth not. Distress and terror drive even atheists to call upon God.... Prayer is an instinct of nature in man, as much so as his love of society. He cannot, he does not live without it, except in a morbid or unnatural state of his mind.

> Diary
> August 14, 1811

Thomas Jefferson
on Religious Instruction

As Rector of the University of Virginia, established in 1819, Thomas Jefferson served as chairman of the governing body, which submitted annual reports to the State Legislature.

In his report of October 7, 1822, Jefferson offered a proposal for religious instruction at the publicly-funded university. He began by referring to an earlier report in which he had been involved:

> In the same report of the commissioners of 1818 [by which a plan for the establishment of the University of Virginia was set forth] it was stated by them that "in conformity with the principles of constitution, which place all sects of religion on an equal footing, with the jealousies of the different sects in guarding that equality from encroachment or surprise, and with the sentiments of the legislature in freedom of religion, manifested on former occasions, they had not proposed that any professorship of divinity should be established in the University; that provision, however, was made for giving instruction in the Hebrew, Greek and Latin languages, the depositories of the originals, and of the earliest and most respected authorities of the faith of every sect, and for courses of ethical lectures, developing those moral obligations in which all sects agree. That, proceeding thus far, without offence to the constitution, they had left, at this point, to every sect to take into their own hands the office of further instruction in the peculiar tenet of each."
>
> It was not, however, to be understood that instruction in religious opinion and duties was

meant to be precluded by the public authorities, as indifferent to the interests of society. On the contrary, the relations which exist between man and his Maker, and the duties resulting from those relations, are the most interesting and important to every human being, and the most incumbent on his study and investigation. The want of instruction in the various creeds of religious faith existing among our citizens presents, therefore, a chasm in a general institution of the useful sciences. But it was thought that this want, and the entrustment to each society of instruction in its own doctrine, were evils of less danger than a permission to the public authorities to dictate modes or principles of religious instruction, or than opportunities furnished them by giving countenance of ascendancy to any one sect over another.

A remedy, however, has been suggested of promising aspect, which, while it excludes the public authorities from the domain of religious freedom, will give to the sectarian schools of divinity the full benefit the public provisions made for instruction in the other branches of science. These branches are equally necessary to the divine as to the other professional or civil characters, to enable them to fulfill the duties of their calling with understanding and usefulness.

It has, therefore, been in contemplation, and suggested by some pious individuals, who perceive the advantages of associating other studies with those of religion, to establish their religious schools on the confines of the University, so as to give to their students ready and convenient access and attendance on the specific lectures of the University; and to maintain, by that means, those destined for the religious professions on as high a standing of science, and of personal weight and respectability, as may be obtained by others from the benefits of the University. Such establishments would offer the further and greater advantage of enabling the students of the University to attend religious exercises with the professor of their particular sect, either in the rooms of the building still to be erected, and destined to that purpose under impartial regulations, as proposed in the same report of the commissioners, or in the lecturing room of such professor.

To such propositions the visitors are disposed to lend a willing ear, and would think it their duty to give every encouragement, by assuring to those who might choose such a location for their schools, that the regulations of the University should be so modified and accommodated as to give every facility of access and attendance to their students, with such regulated use also as may be permitted to the other students, of the library which may hereafter be acquired, either by public or private munificence. But always understanding that these schools shall be independent of the University and of each other.

Such an arrangement would complete the circle of the useful sciences embraced by this institution, and would fill the chasm now existing, on principles which would leave inviolate the constitutional freedom of religion, the most inalienable and sacred of all human rights, over which the people and authorities of this state, individually and publicly, have ever manifested the most watchful jealousy: and could this jealousy be now alarmed, in the opinion of the legislature, by what is here suggested, the idea will be relinquished on any surmise of disapprobation which they might think proper to express.

Would such a relationship between religious institutions and publicly-funded educational facilities be favorably considered today?

Thomas Paine:
Perpetual Agitator

Although never an elected official or a military leader in this country, Thomas Paine made an important contribution to the American Revolution through his timely and forceful writings. *Common Sense*, published in early 1776, set forth the case for American independence in a highly persuasive manner that appealed to the intellectual leadership as well as to the general public. By openly advocating separation from Britain, Paine's pamphlet converted subdued talk of such a possibility into debate about how and when.

Later that year, the first of his three *American Crisis* essays rallied the people: "These are the times that try men's souls." "Tyranny, like hell, is not easily conquered; yet we have the consolation with us that the harder the conflict, the more glorious the triumph."

His thoughts on religion — written some twenty years later in France during the revolution in that country — were published as *The Age of Reason*, causing a general outcry in the United States. As a self-proclaimed Deist, Paine was antagonistic and insulting toward organized religion in general and Christianity in particular. Ironically, his writings reveal that he was motivated by a fervent concern about the relationship between God and human conduct.

Almost two hundred years ago, Thomas Paine — a true extremist in matters of religion — was, nevertheless, critical of the exclusion of God from the educational process. His evaluation of the modern American high school curriculum would be especially interesting.

The God in whom we believe is a God of moral truth .... The practice of moral truth, or, in other words, a practical imitation of the moral goodness of God, is our acting towards each other as He acts benignly towards all .... The only idea we can have of serving God is that of contributing to the happiness of the living creation that God has made.

The Age of Reason, Part I
1793

* * *

Were a man impressed as fully and strongly as he ought to be with the belief of a God, his moral life would be regulated by the force of belief; he would stand in awe of God.

The Age of Reason, Part II
1795

* * *

How is it, that when we study the works of God in the creation, we stop short, and do not think of GOD? It is from the error of the schools in having taught those subjects as accomplishments only, and thereby separated the study of them from the Being who is the author of them.

The Existence of God
1797

The evil that has resulted from the error of the schools, in teaching natural philosophy as an accomplishment only, has been that of generating in the pupils a species of atheism. Instead of looking through the works of creation to the Creator himself, they stop short, and employ the knowledge they acquire to create doubts of His existence.

The Existence of God
1797

* * *

To God, and not to man, are all men to account for their belief.

The Existence of God
1797

There is one point of union wherein all religions meet, and that is in the first article of every man's creed, and of every nation's creed, that has any creed at all: *I believe in God.*

In your first letter [to John Adams] you say, "Let divines and philosophers, statesmen and patriots, unite their endeavors to *renovate the age,* by inculcating in the minds of youth *the fear and love of the Deity and universal philanthropy.*" Why, my dear friend, this is exactly *my* religion, and is the whole of it. That you may have an idea that the *Age of Reason* inculcates this reverential fear and love of the Deity, I will give you a paragraph from it.

"Do we want to contemplate his power? We see it in the immensity of the Creation. Do we want to contemplate his wisdom? We see it in the unchangeable order by which the incomprehensible whole is governed. Do we want to contemplate his munificence? We see it in the abundance with which he fills the earth. Do we want to contemplate his mercy? We see it in his not withholding that abundance even from the unthankful."

As I am fully with you in your first part, that respecting the Deity, so am I in your second, that of *universal philanthropy.*

Letter to Samuel Adams
January 1, 1803

The Test of History

The writings of the individuals who founded this nation revealed their belief that God was an active participant in human history and would assist people who made an honest attempt to conform their behavior to the Divine will and pray for forgiveness and support. They clearly regarded religion and virtue as essential elements in any government based on election of representatives by the general public.

Were they correct only in the technical, secular aspects of government — the useful combination of a bicameral legislature, a single elected executive, and an independent judiciary? Where they wrong in their belief in God, their voluntary support of religion, and their concern for public virtue?

If Americans can agree that the founders of this country were essentially on target in their ideas about government and the organization of society, we cannot now dismiss the other ideas they offered us. If those leaders were suddenly to appear on the scene today, they might well urge — possibly demand — that devotion to God, the study of His intervention in human history, and our close attention to the moral aspect of daily life should be reinstated as positive forces in American society.

Making the Study of American History More Complete – Once Again

We face a dilemma today. The founders of this nation were emphatic in their resistance to the imposition of religious views on individuals or groups by government at any level. Yet at the same time, they encouraged private religion. In fact, they regularly stated their assumption that virtuous principles and the Holy Bible would continue to be important — actually, essential — aspects of the education of every boy and girl in America.

We can bring God, virtue, and Biblical principles back into the classroom in a manner consistent with the beliefs and expectations of those who carried out the American Revolution and produced our Constitution. *Reading the words of our nation's founders during every school day would permit our children to absorb the principles those eminent leaders considered essential to the process of establishing and defending liberty.*

How can we fail to refer to the actual words of our nation's founders, who risked everything and sacrificed mightily to convert their ideas and personal faith into the form of government that we enjoy today? They guided the new nation through the testing and adjustments of the early years and, throughout their retirement years, continued to reflect on their earlier work and the nation's future. Who could provide better guidance for the citizens of the United States today?

Our nation's founders never lost sight of what George Mason and James Madison called "the duty we owe our Creator." And, "with a firm reliance on Divine Providence," they achieved great things for themselves and for us.

We can learn much from them.

Daily Reading of Advice and Prayers Of Our Nation's Founders

The fundamentals of citizenship — with particular emphasis on the spiritual principles that influenced the founders of our nation — should be studied on a continuing basis, in a manner similar to English and math. Memorizing a few important dates and places on certain occasions during twelve years of schooling is insufficient.

John Hancock's signing of the Declaration of Independence on July 4, 1776 is a significant reference point in American history. However, as information for good citizenship, that fact is far less important than a basic sense of the values that motivated the members of the Continental Congress to sever their ties with the British Empire and pledge their "lives, fortunes, and sacred honor" to make good their commitment. A brief daily reminder of the beliefs of the men who established the United States of America will enable every student to recognize and remember that our nation's government is based on religious precepts.

It is worth noting that the delegates to the Continental Congress did not sign the parchment copy, now in the National Archives of the United States, until August 2, 1776. However, John Hancock, as President of the Congress, and Charles Thomson, as Secretary, evidently affixed their signatures to a copy of the final wording that had been "agreed to" in Committee of the Whole on July 4, 1776. Printed copies were distributed the next day over their names set in type.

A vote of the delegates on *July 2* had approved the resolution for independence introduced the previous month by Richard Henry Lee — causing John

239

Adams to speculate that in the future July 2 would be celebrated as the primary national holiday. Even such apparently straightforward "facts" as the signing of the Declaration of Independence and deciding which day to commemorate are often a bit more complex than generally recognized.

Observing the Fourth of July as Independence Day each year focuses on a single highly symbolic moment, simplifying what actually was a complex, dynamic series of events that most of us understand only vaguely. Yet our annual celebration sparks a sense of respect and gratitude — a reminder of the fight for independence and the struggle to build a new nation.

Similarly, a daily reading of the advice and prayers of the founders will provide us with awareness that reverence for God exerted a major influence on the formation of the government we enjoy today. We do not need a detailed understanding of the religious beliefs of each individual — or a perfect memory of their exact words — to recognize that God, religion and virtue were important to the men who established this country.

Advice for Today

Do words written more than two hundred years ago have any relevance today? How can the advice and prayers of our nation's founders apply to the problems of the late twentieth century?

With amazing inconsistency, we Americans rely on intensive analysis of each word and phrase of the Constitution of the United States to define our freedom *from* one thing and another — yet we neglect the urging of the founders for us to love God and seek the virtuous path. If they were so wise in establishing our present form of government, why do we reject their wisdom with respect to prayer and morality?

Even though construction techniques have changed significantly during the last two hundred years, most of us would respect the written advice of the designers and builders of a house that has stood since 1776. And common sense dictates that weakening the foundation of any structure is perilous — unless, of course, destruction is intended.

The designers and builders of our form of government clearly described its foundation: reverence for God. We would be well advised to heed their advice and make certain that the foundation is strong enough to support today's house of government, which is much larger than that anticipated in the original plans.

Timeline 1725 - 1850

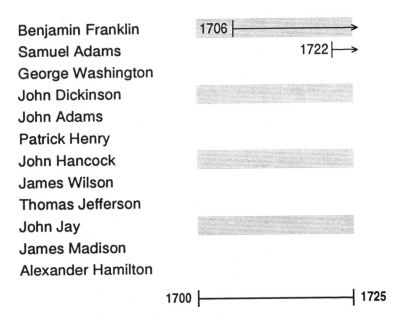

Benjamin Franklin	1706
Samuel Adams	1722
George Washington	
John Dickinson	
John Adams	
Patrick Henry	
John Hancock	
James Wilson	
Thomas Jefferson	
John Jay	
James Madison	
Alexander Hamilton	

1700 — 1725

The timeline that begins on this page illustrates the relative age of the founders of our nation. For example, Benjamin Franklin was born in 1706, nearly fifty years before Alexander Hamilton (1755). Yet both Franklin and Hamilton were active in the Patriot cause during the most critical years of the formation of the United States: from the movement for independence through ratification of the Constitution.

The period of each individual's significant involvement in civic and governmental affairs is indicated by ★★★★★ in his timeline. Benjamin Franklin was appointed Clerk (Secretary) of the Pennsylvania Assembly (Legislature) in 1736 and continued to play an important role in American politics until 1788. Alexander Hamilton was barely in his twenties in 1776, when he was appointed commander of a company of artillery. Therefore, his civic and governmental involvement began well after that of Benjamin Franklin, but continued beyond Franklin's death — even though Hamilton's life, which ended in a pistol duel with Aaron Burr (then Vice President of the United States), was shorter than that of any other major founder of our nation.

Timeline 1725 - 1850

A 1732 Georgia, the thirteenth British colony between Canada and Spanish Florida, is settled.

B 1733 Molasses Act, a heavy British tax on American trade, becomes law but is loosely enforced.

C 1754 French and Indian War against the British Colonies in America begins.

D 1760 British forces capture Montreal, effectively ending the French and Indian War.

E 1765 Stamp Act Congress asserts the right of the American Colonies to regulate their own affairs (in reaction to new British taxes).

F 1770 British troops fire on townspeople, killing three, in the "Boston Massacre."

G 1773 British tea is dumped into the harbor in the "Boston Tea Party."

H 1775 Massachusetts militia (the "Minutemen") clash with British troops at Lexington and Concord.

Timeline 1725 - 1850

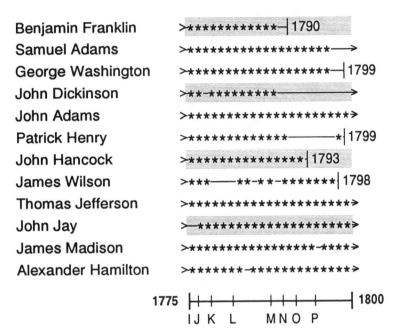

Benjamin Franklin	>***********—	1790
Samuel Adams	>*******************—→	
George Washington	>*******************—	1799
John Dickinson	>**–********——————→	
John Adams	>********************>	
Patrick Henry	>*************————*|	1799
John Hancock	>***************|	1793
James Wilson	>***——**-* *-********|	1798
Thomas Jefferson	>********************>	
John Jay	>*********************>	
James Madison	>*****************–****>	
Alexander Hamilton	>*******–*************>	

1775 ├─┼─┼──┼──┼─┼──┼─┤ 1800
       IJ K L   MNO P

I	1775	George Washington becomes commander-in-chief of the newly authorized Continental Army.
J	1776	Declaration of Independence is approved and signed by the Continental Congress.
K	1778	Continental Army, emerging from a brutal winter at Valley Forge, renews fight for independence.
L	1781	British force in Virginia surrenders, effectively ending the Revolutionary War.
M	1787	Constitution of the United States is approved by a special convention and submitted to the States for ratification.
N	1789	George Washington becomes the first President under the Constitution; the first Congress convenes; the Supreme Court is created.
O	1791	Bill of Rights, consisting of ten amendments to the Constitution, is ratified.
P	1794	Jay Treaty with Britain ends threat of a new war, but sparks violent pro-French protests.

Timeline 1725 - 1850

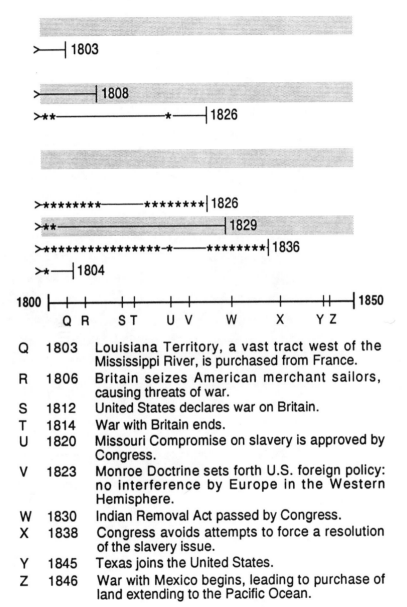

Q   1803   Louisiana Territory, a vast tract west of the Mississippi River, is purchased from France.
R   1806   Britain seizes American merchant sailors, causing threats of war.
S   1812   United States declares war on Britain.
T   1814   War with Britain ends.
U   1820   Missouri Compromise on slavery is approved by Congress.
V   1823   Monroe Doctrine sets forth U.S. foreign policy: no interference by Europe in the Western Hemisphere.
W   1830   Indian Removal Act passed by Congress.
X   1838   Congress avoids attempts to force a resolution of the slavery issue.
Y   1845   Texas joins the United States.
Z   1846   War with Mexico begins, leading to purchase of land extending to the Pacific Ocean.

Brief Biographies

Of Our Nation's Founders

Benjamin Franklin

1706 - 1790

Successful businessman, clever writer, inventor of practical devices, and a highly respected scientist, Benjamin Franklin was the first American whose accomplishments were widely recognized in Europe at the same time that they were acclaimed in his own part of the world. His self-made wealth was sufficient for him to retire from business in his early forties.

Concerned about the affairs of government in America, he was active in the Pennsylvania Assembly and represented several of the Colonies as an agent in London, England. While there, he repeatedly tried to negotiate a reconciliation between Britain and the Patriot cause. When a peaceful settlement proved impossible, he came home to sign the Declaration of Independence. More than ten years later, serving as a delegate to the Constitutional Convention at age 81, he made the motion to approve the Constitution of the United States.

His printing and publishing business — which included one of Philadelphia's first newspapers and twenty-six editions of *Poor Richard's Almanac* — enabled him to express his opinions to a large audience and brought him in touch with many of the leaders in America. His fifteen years of service as Clerk of the Pennsylvania Assembly and his position as Postmaster of Philadelphia extended his range of political and business contacts. He was the prime mover in the founding of the American Philosophical Society, which served as a forum for many of the most ingenious minds in the Colonies and, eventually, in the United States.

His inventions ranged from the Franklin Stove and the lightning rod to bifocal lenses and an exotic musical instrument (the glass armonica) for which Wolfgang Amadeus Mozart wrote a concerto.

The motives behind Franklin's proposal to open each session of the Continental Congress with a prayer have been questioned because it was offered when the delegates were mired in controversy and the entire effort to form a new American government was in jeopardy. But could there have been a better time for prayer? In his old age, Benjamin Franklin made a special point of recalling that, as a young man, he had recognized the importance of worshipping God and had thereupon begun a lifetime effort of moral improvement.

Samuel Adams

1722 - 1803

Samuel Adams, a Boston brewer and tax collector with a Master of Arts degree from Harvard, was the most thoroughly committed revolutionary among our nation's founders. Even when Britain temporarily reduced the severity of its taxation of the Colonies, inducing other American leaders to become quiet, Sam Adams maintained his relentless criticism of British policies as a means of agitating for complete self-determination.

The writings of Samuel Adams, both as resolutions prepared for town meetings and in the form of newspaper correspondence, were widely read, with particular impact in New England. His speeches in Boston and environs rivaled the intensity of Patrick Henry's orations in Virginia. In concert with his cousin, the lawyer John Adams, he set forth the demands of Massachusetts with great effectiveness.

"Sammy the Maltster," as he was called by his political opponents, was the major force in energizing dissent in the streets of Boston and organizing mass protests in support of the Patriot cause. A signer of the Declaration of Independence, he was active in the Continental Congress during the Revolutionary War.

More adept at agitation than developing structures of government, he did not attend the Constitutional Convention. However, during the Massachusetts convention to consider ratification of the Constitution of the United States, he voiced his concern that the Federal government might wield oppressive power over ordinary citizens and insisted that personal and local rights be guaranteed through future amendments. Most of his objections were ultimately incorporated in the Bill of Rights.

Samuel Adams was a force in Massachusetts politics throughout his later years, helping to prepare the State Constitution and serving as President of the Massachusetts Senate. He was elected Lieutenant-Governor of Massachusetts, serving under his political rival, John Hancock, and became Governor upon Hancock's early death. Elected Governor the next year, Adams served his four-year term and retired from public service.

George Washington

1732 - 1799

As both the military leader and the most visible symbol of the American Revolution, George Washington became the steadying force of the new United States of America. His solid presence held together the ragged Continental Army at Valley Forge in the brutal winter of 1777-78 — and for six more years. His imperturbable image was required again at Philadelphia, four years after the peace treaty with Britain that assured genuine independence for the United States, in order to sustain the difficult process of preparing a new Constitution that would bind the thirteen quarreling States into one nation.

When the time came to elect a President to establish the executive branch of government, there was no other choice but George Washington. By unanimous vote of the representatives of the fledgling federal republic, he was drafted at age 56 to serve as our first President for four stressful years ... and then for four more.

"Father of his country." "First in war, first in peace, and first in the hearts of his countrymen." George Washington fulfilled his role with an extraordinary calmness based on a sense of destiny. Throughout his military battles, beginning in his early twenties, he escaped serious injury in the most remarkable manner. From that time forward, he was always willing to answer his country's call — even though, in many respects, he was more concerned about assaults on his motives and his character during civilian service to his government than about the physical attacks that had been directed against his very life during wartime. Ultimately, he relied on the help of God to see him through.

George Washington's major contribution as the nation's first President was his ability to maintain a middle course among competing factions — based on his determination that the United States should remain a true Union, while resisting the demands of foreign alliances. He repeatedly warned against "factionalism." Interestingly, the two-party system that emerged during his administration ultimately became an important part of the "checks and balances" of American government.

John Dickinson

1732 - 1808

John Dickinson was known as "the Penman of the Revolution" for his early and extensive writings that asserted the rights of the American Colonies. His involvement in Patriotic affairs began with participation in the Stamp Act Congress of 1765. His essays, letters, and petitions — even a popular "Liberty Song" — rallied the American cause. He served in the Continental Congress, where he opposed the Declaration of Independence as premature in 1776, but was called upon to draft the Articles of Confederation immediately thereafter. Ten years later, he played an important role in the Constitutional Convention of 1787.

Dickinson was reluctant to accept the idea of outright separation from Britain. Nevertheless, once the decision was made by the majority of the delegates, he supported the new United States and was frequently elected to public office. He also served briefly in the Continental army, first as a general in the militia and later as a volunteer private.

As a major property owner in both Pennsylvania and Delaware, John Dickinson was eligible to serve in public office in either State. He became President of the Supreme Executive Council — in effect, Governor — of Delaware in 1781 and held the same position in Pennsylvania between 1782 and 1785. Soon thereafter, he returned to Delaware, which would be his home for the remainder of his life.

His participation in the Constitutional Convention — and in the Delaware Convention that was the first to ratify the Constitution — contributed much to adoption of our present form of government. Beyond his official public service, he also urged ratification of the Constitution by other States in his widely read and persuasive essays, signed "Fabius," which were later published in book form.

John Dickinson then returned to private life, but maintained an active interest in the development of the new American republic and frequently contributed essays on subjects relating to government and education.

John Adams

1735 - 1826

Throughout his life, John Adams was a determined advocate. He became a successful Boston lawyer, capable of representing either side in a controversy — first defending a Massachusetts businessman (John Hancock) accused of smuggling in defiance of British import regulations, then defending the British troops who fired on a Boston mob that had been protesting those same regulations. However, his fundamental commitment to the rights of the Colonists made him an early spokesman for independence and caused him to devote his remaining years to public service. He believed that the ordinary citizen, with a proper education, would be the foundation of a grand new system of government in America.

From the initial stirrings of revolution, when he asserted the rights of the Colonists during the Stamp Act crisis in Boston, to the signing of the Declaration of Independence in Philadelphia, John Adams was a leader in the formal conventions and assemblies in Massachusetts — while his cousin Samuel organized the people in the streets to oppose the British presence.

After serving as a diplomat for the United States in Europe during the Revolutionary War, John Adams became the second President of the United States. He soon found that George Washington was an especially difficult act to follow.

During his previous eight years as Vice President, Adams had become the head of the Federalist party, a political faction that disagreed — often bitterly — with the ideas of the Democratic-Republicans, led by Secretary of State Thomas Jefferson. The Federalists, generally supported by George Washington, favored a strong role for the central government, while Jefferson's Democratic-Republicans leaned toward the reservation of rights to the States. As in most political parties, internal disputes developed among the Federalists, and criticism by Alexander Hamilton, the Federalist leader in New York, contributed to a narrow loss by Adams in his bid for a second term as President.

In his retirement, John Adams reestablished his early friendship with Thomas Jefferson, who succeeded him in the Presidency. Their correspondence, particularly with respect to religion, was remarkable.

Patrick Henry

1736 - 1799

A largely self-taught country lawyer, Patrick Henry used his power of reasoning and oratory to make a prominent place for himself in Colonial Virginia, where property and social status were ordinarily required to gain favorable attention. Within three years of obtaining his license to practice law (after only a few months of study), Henry successfully argued a highly significant case in which he convinced a jury that a Virginia law was valid without the consent of the British King — a revolutionary concept in 1763. Two years later, he persuaded the Virginia House of Burgesses to lend support to his assertion that the Stamp Act passed by the British Parliament was unconstitutional. His opponents branded his passionate remarks during the debate "treason."

Although his challenge to the Virginia Convention in 1775 — "Give me liberty or give me death!" — is one of the ringing phrases of the American Revolution that carried throughout the thirteen Colonies, Patrick Henry confined virtually all of his political activity to his home government. However, he did attend the Continental Congress for one session, where he joined in a successful push to establish the Continental Army. Elected the first Governor of Virginia under the Constitution of 1776, he served in that capacity or as a member of the Virginia Legislature for most of the next dozen years before returning to the practice of law.

Growing increasingly conservative, Patrick Henry proposed the reintroduction of State taxation to support churches in Virginia, a move that was successfully blocked through the persuasiveness of an essay and petition written by James Madison. Henry also opposed ratification of the Constitution of the United States — which had the outspoken support of fellow Virginians George Washington, Thomas Jefferson and James Madison — because he feared that centralized authority would be abused. James Madison, who shared Henry's concern for protection of individual and local rights, would soon lead the effort in Congress to assure passage of the Bill of Rights, which met many of Henry's objections. After the battle over the Constitution, Patrick Henry gradually withdrew from public service and returned to private life.

John Hancock

1737 - 1793

Consistent with his bold signature on the Declaration of Independence, John Hancock played an important symbolic, as well as practical, role throughout the period of the American Revolution. His wealth and privileged social position in Colonial Boston made him a well-known figure — multiplying the effect of his protests against the Stamp Act, his trial on charges of smuggling for defiance of British taxes on American imports, and his dramatic oration at the funeral of citizens killed by British troops in the "Boston Massacre."

By 1775, John Hancock, the aristocrat, and Samuel Adams, the public agitator (yet, like Hancock, a Harvard man), were the two American leaders sought by the British on charges of high treason. A warning from Paul Revere enabled them to escape from Boston and serve as delegates to the Continental Congress, where Hancock was elected President. In that capacity, he was the first member to sign the Declaration of Independence.

During the Revolutionary War, John Hancock continued his service in Congress and, as an officer in the Continental Army, participated in an unsuccessful military campaign in New England. After the war, he returned to popular acclaim in Massachusetts. The first Governor elected under the Massachusetts Constitution of 1780, he served in that office, interrupted only by a term in the United States Congress, continuously until his death at age 56.

James Wilson

1742 - 1798

Bringing his Scottish sense of independence to America, James Wilson quickly became a leading lawyer in Philadelphia. He was accused of pro-British leanings because many of his clients were Tories, but he consistently advocated the right of ordinary American citizens to participate directly in the selection of their representatives in government. His broad knowledge of history and his talent for constitutional law gave his views considerable power in the Continental Congress and the Constitutional Convention. In fact, he was one of only six individuals who signed both the Declaration of Independence and the Constitution of the United States.

In 1774, two years before the Declaration of Independence, James Wilson wrote a widely read pamphlet that challenged the authority of the British Parliament to regulate the American Colonies, an argument that suggested the need for self-determination by the legislatures on this side of the Atlantic. As a member of the Continental Congress, he voted for independence — in opposition to the desire for further negotiation expressed by his former mentor and fellow Pennsylvanian, John Dickinson.

In the Constitutional Convention, James Wilson was an important force in advocating and clarifying legal concepts and structures. He strongly promoted popular election of the members of Congress and the President of the United States — a radical concept in many areas of the country at that time. In addition, he served as the spokesman for Benjamin Franklin, the senior statesman of the convention at age 81.

James Wilson also played a significant role in securing Pennsylvania's ratification of the Constitution. Although he was regarded by the general public as an elitist, he strongly supported the rights of the people to participate directly in the choice of their national representatives. His work in drafting a new Pennsylvania Constitution, approved in 1790, helped to broaden voting rights and liberalize the requirements for holding office in that State.

At age 47, James Wilson was appointed by President Washington to become one of five Associate Justices on the first Supreme Court of the United States. Within a few years thereafter, his financial affairs deteriorated rapidly as a result of previous land speculation. Pressured by creditors, he died suddenly at age 56 in the home of another member of the Supreme Court.

Thomas Jefferson

1743 - 1826

One individual accepted responsibility for converting the passions, grievances, dreams, and concepts of government held by of our country's founders into a single document. In 1776, at age 33, Thomas Jefferson drafted the Declaration of Independence for the Continental Congress, representing the thirteen Colonies that would soon become the United States. Blending his interpretation of the writings of European thinkers with guidance and comments from a distinguished committee that included Benjamin Franklin and John Adams, he completed that enduring work in less than a month. His words, which capture the spirit of the American Revolution and the determination of the Patriots to establish a system of government based on the aspirations of the people, have been quoted by political movements around the world since that time.

Thomas Jefferson's public service continued throughout his life. He was a leading advocate for religious freedom in his home state of Virginia, represented his country as ambassador to France, accepted George Washington's offer to become the first Secretary of State, and served two terms as President of the United States. In his retirement years, he led the effort to establish the University of Virginia and served as its Rector. His interests ranged well beyond government and education to encompass architecture, scientific farming, paleontology, botany and an intensive study of the Bible.

While a member of President Washington's cabinet, Thomas Jefferson engaged in frequent and increasingly bitter controversies with Secretary of the Treasury Alexander Hamilton, leading to the development of the American two-party system.

Once Thomas Jefferson became President, he began to see the need for action by the national government in certain situations — despite his earlier criticism of the Federalists who preceded him. During his first term, he carried out the Louisiana Purchase, acquiring for the United States an immense territory without the approval of Congress — or of the States, whose rights he had stanchly defended as a Democratic-Republican. His second four years in office were dominated by efforts to avoid involvement in the frequent wars between Britain and France. Unfortunately, by prohibiting foreign trade to achieve that objective, he caused economic hardship in many areas of the country. Although his political party maintained its dominance in national politics, Jefferson followed Washington's example and declined to seek a third term as President.

John Jay

1745 - 1829

A conservative, well-connected lawyer at the beginning of the movement toward American independence, John Jay became an important spokesman for the Patriot cause, serving as President of the Continental Congress during a portion of the Revolutionary War. In 1776, he helped form the newly independent government of New York by drafting the state constitution.

During the war for independence, he was sent to Europe by Congress, first in a frustrating attempt to reach an agreement with Spain, followed by more successful service as a commissioner (supporting Benjamin Franklin and John Adams) in the peace conference between the United States and Britain. Upon returning to this country, he was appointed Secretary for Foreign Affairs.

Perhaps John Jay's greatest contribution to the new nation was his persuasive writing in favor of ratification of the Constitution of the United States. He joined Alexander Hamilton and James Madison in contributing a highly important series of newspaper essays (compiled and widely circulated as a book, *The Federalist*), which made a persuasive case for approval. He then backed up his ideas through political activities in the New York Convention.

As early as 1777, John Jay was prominent in American judicial affairs as the first Chief Justice of the Supreme Court of New York. More than ten years later, he was appointed the first Chief Justice of the Supreme Court of the United States by President George Washington. While serving in that capacity, he was designated a special ambassador to Britain for the purpose of averting a new war between the nations. He negotiated a largely inconclusive treaty that failed to alter the British practice of seizing American merchant seamen but did provide for the withdrawal of British troops from the Northwest Territory. The agreement caused him to be bitterly denounced by the majority of Americans, who favored the side of France in the basic dispute with Britain. Upon returning once again to New York, he resigned his position on the Supreme Court of the United States to become Governor of his home State.

In his later years, John Jay devoted much of his time and energy to the American Bible Society.

James Madison

1751 - 1836

At age 36, James Madison became the central figure in the development of the Constitution of the United States. He achieved that distinction by means of preparation — an extensive study of the theory of governmental structures in relation to practical outcomes in human history — which he combined with skillful presentation and dedication to the task of building an American nation. Throughout the Constitutional Convention, he recorded the key arguments on both sides of every significant issue, enabling him to formulate written solutions to many of the most difficult problems during preparation of the final document.

Madison was elected to represent Virginia in the House of Representatives in the first Congress of the United States convened under the newly ratified Constitution. He promptly guided the Bill of Rights — the first ten amendments — through the Congressional approval process, thus fulfilling promises in various state conventions (particularly Massachusetts, New York and Virginia) that individual liberties would be guaranteed.

He was appointed Secretary of State in Thomas Jefferson's administration, then was elected to two terms as the fourth President of the United States. The War of 1812, which began toward the end of his first administration, was almost entirely unsatisfactory in terms of international objectives, but it became a public relations victory through late military triumphs, including Andrew Jackson's defeat of the British at New Orleans after the peace treaty had been signed. After retiring from elective office, Madison worked closely with Thomas Jefferson in helping to establish the University of Virginia and became Rector after Jefferson's death.

His theological studies at the College of New Jersey (now Princeton University) and his observations of sectarian intolerance upon his return to Virginia contributed to Madison's sensitivity to religious issues — and his lifelong attention to the separation of church and state. He took action to block or reverse any governmental action that would give one religious denomination an advantage over any other. At the same time, he evidently shared the prevailing assumption of his day that the manner of worshipping and serving God would continue to be of deepest concern to American citizens. It is doubtful that he even contemplated a society in which the government and its educational establishment would make a systematic effort to separate learning from morality and reverence of God.

Alexander Hamilton

1755 - 1804

A brilliant but apparently difficult person, Alexander Hamilton played a major role in defining and promoting our American system of government — yet he never held a major elective office.

As a teenager, Hamilton helped to persuade the citizens of New York to support the Patriot cause and commanded a company of artillery in the Continental Army. In his early twenties, he was a key member of General George Washington's staff during the Revolutionary War.

Although the inadequacy of the Articles of Confederation (adopted during the war as a means of coordinating the activities of the United States) had become painfully apparent within a short time, Alexander Hamilton was among the few politicians willing to call for extensive changes to remedy the defects of the old agreement. The Constitutional Convention in Philadelphia gave him the opportunity to promote his ideas for a strong central government.

The ultimate compromise with those who wished to reserve most rights for the States was acceptable to Hamilton. Because ratification by the State conventions was uncertain at best, he and James Madison of Virginia became aggressive advocates for approval of the new Constitution of the United States. In a series of newspaper essays, which were quickly published (together with important contributions by John Jay) in book form as *The Federalist*, their writings proved effective, helping to secure ratification.

Soon thereafter, Hamilton was appointed the first Secretary of the Treasury by President George Washington. He successfully proposed numerous measures for extending the powers of the Federal government in taxation, banking and foreign trade, intending to promote domestic prosperity through centralized action. Some of his ideas proved beneficial; others did not. His often acrimonious disagreements with Secretary of State Thomas Jefferson, who generally favored the rights of the States, led to the development of the American two-party system.

Hamilton resigned from the Cabinet after six years of service. His successful effort to thwart Aaron Burr's political ambitions led to a pistol duel in which Vice-President Burr ended Alexander Hamilton's life at age 49.

Sources

ADAMS, ABIGAIL

Butterfield, L. H. (Editor). *Adams Family Correspondence* [1963]

ADAMS, JOHN

Adams, Charles Francis. *Life of John Adams* [1850]

Adams, Charles Francis (Editor). *Works of John Adams* [1850]

Butterfield, L. H. (Editor). *Adams Family Correspondence* [1963]

Butterfield, L. H. (Editor). *Diary and Autobiography of John Adams* [1961]

Cappon, Lester J. (Editor). *Adams-Jefferson Letters* [1988]

Poore, Benjamin Perley (Editor). *Federal and State Constitutions, Colonial Charters, and Other Organic Laws of The United States* [1877]

Richardson, James D. (Editor). *Messages and Papers of the Presidents* [1911]

Taylor, Robert J. (Editor). *Papers of John Adams* [1979]

ADAMS, SAMUEL

Cushing, Harry Alonzo (Editor). *Writings of Samuel Adams* [1904, 1968]

ALLEN, ETHAN

_____. *A Narrative of Colonial Ethan Allen's Captivity* [1779, 1807]

Pell, John. *Ethan Allen* [1929]

BOUDINOT, ELIAS

Smith, Paul H. (Editor). *Letters of Delegates to Congress 1774-1789* [1976]

CARROLL, CHARLES

Field, Thomas Meagher (Editor). *Unpublished Letters of Charles Carroll of Carrollton* [1902]

273

CONTINENTAL CONGRESS
Library of Congress, Manuscript Division (various editors). *Journals of the Continental Congress 1774-1789* [1904-1937]

DICKINSON, JOHN
_____. *Political Writings* [1801]

Library of Congress, Manuscript Division (various editors). *Journals of the Continental Congress 1774-1789* [1904-1937]

Historical Society of Pennsylvania. R. R. Logan Manuscript Collection

FRANKLIN, BENJAMIN
Fay, Bernard. *Franklin, The Apostle of Modern Times* [1929]

Franklin Institute, The. *Benjamin Franklin: Quotable Quotes* [n.d. 1956?]

Poore, Benjamin Perley (Editor). *Federal and State Constitutions, Colonial Charters, and Other Organic Laws of The United States* [1877]

Smyth, Albert Henry (Editor). *Writings of Benjamin Franklin* [1907]

Stevenson, Burton (Editor). *Home Book of Proverbs* [1967]

HAMILTON, ALEXANDER
Lodge, Henry Cabot (Editor). *Works of Alexander Hamilton* [1904]

Syrett, Harold C. (Editor). *Papers of Alexander Hamilton* [1974]

HANCOCK, JOHN
Brown, Abram English. *John Hancock: His Book* [1898]

Fowler, William M. *Baron of Beacon Hill* [1980]

Wagner, Frederick. *Patriot's Choice: The Story of John Hancock* [1964]

HENRY, PATRICK
Wirt, William. *Sketches of the Life and Character of Patrick Henry* [1854]

IREDELL, JAMES

McRee, Griffith J. *Life and Correspondence of James Iredell* [1949]

JAY, JOHN

Hough, Franklin Benjamin (Editor). *Proclamations for Thanksgiving* [1858]

Jay, William. *Life of John Jay* [1833, 1972]

Johnston, Henry P. (Editor). *Correspondence and Public Papers of John Jay* [1890]

JEFFERSON, THOMAS

Bergh, A. E. (Editor). *Writings of Thomas Jefferson* [1903, 1907]

Boyd, Julian P. (Editor). *Papers of Thomas Jefferson* [1950]

Library of Congress, Manuscript Division (various editors). *Journals of the Continental Congress 1774-1789* [1904-1937]

Randolph, Thomas Jefferson. *Memoir, Correspondence and Miscellanies from the Papers of Thomas Jefferson* [1830]

Richardson, James D. (Editor). *Messages and Papers of the Presidents* [1911]

Washington, H. A. (Editor). *Writings of Thomas Jefferson* [1854]

LEE, RICHARD HENRY

Ballagh, James, Curtis (Editor). *Letters of Richard Henry Lee* [1914]

MADISON, JAMES

_____. *Letters and Other Writings* [1884]

Brant, Irving. "Two Neglected Madison Letters," *William and Mary Quarterly*, Third Series, Volume 3 [1946]

Farrand, Max (Editor). *Records of the Federal Convention of 1787* [1927]

Hutchinson, William T., and Rachal, William M. E. (Editors). *Papers of James Madison* [1962]

Richardson, James D. (Editor). *Messages and Papers of the Presidents* [1911]

275

Rutland, Robert A. and Mason, Thomas A. (Editors). *Papers of James Madison: Presidential Series* [1984]

MASON, GEORGE
Rutland, Robert A. (Editor). *Papers of George Mason 1725-1792* [1970]

MASSACHUSETTS
Poore, Benjamin Perley (Editor). *Federal and State Constitutions, Colonial Charters, and Other Organic Laws of The United States* [1877]

MORRIS, ROBERT
Johnston, Henry P. (Editor). *Correspondence and Public Papers of John Jay* [1890]

MUHLENBERG, HENRY MELCHIOR
Tappert, Theodore G. and Doberstein, John W. (Editors). *Notebook of a Colonial Clergyman* [1959]

OTIS, JAMES
Bailyn, Bernard (Editor). *Pamphlets of the American Revolution 1750-1776* [1965]

PAINE, THOMAS
Conway, Moncure Daniel (Editor). *Writings of Thomas Paine* [1899]

PENNSYLVANIA
Poore, Benjamin Perley (Editor). *Federal and State Constitutions, Colonial Charters, and Other Organic Laws of The United States* [1877]

RUSH, BENJAMIN
_____. *Essays: Literary, Moral, and Philosophical* [1798]

Butterfield, L. H. (Editor). *Letters of Benjamin Rush* [1951]

Corner, George W. (Editor). *Autobiography of Benjamin Rush* [1948]

SENATE, UNITED STATES

Richardson, James D. (Editor). *Messages and Papers of the Presidents* [1911]

SUFFOLK COUNTY, MASSACHUSETTS

Library of Congress, Manuscript Division (various editors). *Journals of the Continental Congress 1774-1789* [1904-1937]

WASHINGTON, GEORGE

Abbot, W. W. (Editor). *Papers of Washington* [1983]

Fitzpatrick, John C. (Editor). *Writings of Washington* [1932]

Richardson, James D. (Editor). *Messages and Papers of the Presidents* [1911]

WASHINGTON COUNTY, NEW YORK

Jay, William. *Life of John Jay* [1833, 1972]

WILSON, JAMES

McCloskey, Robert Green (Editor). *Works of James Wilson* [1967]

Index

281

Custom editions of this book can be prepared for educational, civic and religious organizations. Also, price discounts on orders of multiple copies are available. If you have a special requirement or would like further information, please contact:

Reading Books
526 Washington Street
P. O. Box 1456
Reading, PA 19603-1456

(800) 577-2788

Illustrations of our nation's founders courtesy of the Print and Picture Department, Free Library of Philadelphia.

Historical timeline by Steven Henderson

Cover art by Tiger Graphics
(prepared by Lori Martin)

Printed by Wickersham Printing Co., Inc.
(with special thanks to Rose Huber)